# Reading

# along with

# Laura Ingalls

# in the

# Big Wisconsin Woods

By Dan L. White

## Reading along with Laura Ingalls in the Big Wisconsin Woods

Published by Ashley Preston Publishing
Hartville, Mo. 65667

www.danlwhitebooks.com

Cover photo from iStock.com, designed by Dan L. White Books staff.

Printed in the United States of America.

Little House is a registered trademark of HarperCollins Publishers Inc.

Scripture quotations from the King James Version (KJV) and the World English Bible (WEB) are in the public domain.

ISBN 13: 978-1495313196
ISBN 10: 1495313190

# Table of Contents

# Other Books by Dan L. White

See page 159 for descriptions

The Jubilee Principle: *God's Plan for Economic Freedom*

Laura's Love Story: *The lifetime love of Laura and Almanzo Wilder*

The Long, Hard Winter of 1880-81 – What was it Really Like?

Laura Ingalls' Friends Remember Her

Devotionals with Laura: *Laura Ingalls' Favorite Bible Selections*

Laura Ingalls Wilder's Most Inspiring Writings

Big Bible Lessons from Laura Ingalls' Little Books

The Real Laura Ingalls: *Who was Real, What was Real on her Prairie TV Show*

Reading along with Laura Ingalls at her Kansas Prairie Home

Homeschool Happenings, Happenstance & Happiness

Tebows' Homeschooled! Should You?

School Baals: *How an Old Idol with a New Name Sneaked into Your School*

Wifely Wisdom for Sometimes Foolish Husbands

Life Lessons from Jane Austen's Pride and Prejudice

Daring to Love like God: *Marriage as a Spiritual Union*

# Reading along with Laura Ingalls in the Big Wisconsin Woods

## Chapter 1 *(Little House in the Big Woods)*

## Big Fire in the Big Woods

*Impression, Sunrise*
By Claude Monet

Many years ago
a little old lady sat down
to write down her memories
of many years ago.

That lady, Laura Ingalls Wilder, began writing her books around 1930, but the time she wrote about was sixty years before then. As she wrote with a number two pencil at her farm near Mansfield, Missouri, her lined tablet was illuminated by electric lights, but that pencil wrote about a time with only dim oil lamps. To buy her tablets and pencils, she rode to town in a gasoline powered motorcar, but she told of riding in buggies and sleds behind frisky horses. When she looked out her window in the Ozarks, she usually saw mild and pleasant weather, while her stories relived the fierce winters and dreadful droughts of the northern Midwest.

Laura's first book did not become famous. Actually, it was never more than a manuscript, because it was never published during her lifetime. That manuscript was titled *Pioneer Girl*, and *Pioneer Girl* recounted the facts of Laura's life.

However, it did not show the spirit of her life.

Not all artists paint a scene exactly as it appears. Some paint like a photograph, but others paint with more feeling than a photograph shows. For example, French impressionist painter Claude Monet's famous painting *Impression, Sunrise* is a beautiful painting of a sunrise, but it focuses more on the feeling of the morning rather than the exactness of each physical detail.

Each of Laura Ingalls Wilder's books is a literary work based on the facts of her life, but shaped into a story that better expresses the tone and color of her life.

Not every detail, then, in Laura's books matches every detail of her life.

Nor could it be that way.

She was an old woman, remembering the long ago time when she was only a tiny girl. What were you doing on this day of the year when you were five years old? No one can accurately remember all details of earliest life. History students of today may actually know more factoids about Laura's life than she did, but they do not know her life as she did. Just as an artist, then, may decline to paint a picture as a photograph, so Laura adjusted some details of her life to better show the story of her life.

And the story of her life is not just the facts of moving from Wisconsin to Kansas to Minnesota to South Dakota. The real story of her life is Pa fiddling in the firelight, Ma teaching her girls manners and deportment, Laura walking in the prairie flowers with beloved sister Mary…

The real story of Laura's life is the love, faith, and happiness of the Ingalls family.

Think about it. What do you remember most about Laura's books?

Historical details?

Or –

Love and happiness?

What most people remember from Laura's books is not just the year that the Ingalls left the big woods, but the warm feeling of knowing that wonderful family in the big woods.

Laura's books are not primarily history books. Since they are often taken as such, she once said, *"I did not realize that I was writing history."*[1]

The Little House books are artistic tales, as if we are sitting around a campfire with Laura, and she wants to keep us interested, so that we will hear her story.

Laura first tried to tell her life's story simply as a factual history. That manuscript was received as most history books are.

But when she and her daughter Rose went back to the campfire and artistically repainted her life story – then we all listened.

There is only one book *Little House in the Big Woods*, of course, but Laura actually lived in the big woods of Wisconsin twice in her young life.

First, when she was born there.

*"I was born in a log house within 4 miles of the legend haunted Lake Pipin in Wisconsin,"* Laura wrote in 1918. *"I remember seeing deer that my father had killed, hanging in the trees about our forest home. When I was four years old we traveled to the Indian Territory, Fort Scott, Kan., being our nearest town. My childish memories hold the sound of the war whoop and I see pictures of painted Indians."*[2]

Laura wrote that article more than a decade before she wrote her first book, and she slightly misremembered how old she was when they moved to Kansas. Laura was born in 1867 and the Wisconsin Historical Society notes that *"The Ingalls left Pepin for Kansas in 1869 but returned two years later."*[3]

When Laura was only two years old, then, Pa Ingalls sold their big woods farm and bought a place in Missouri. Soon after that, Pa sold the Missouri property and the family moved on to the Kansas prairie. A couple of years later, they moved back to Wisconsin and the buyer of their farm there let them have it back. Then they lived in Wisconsin for four more years.

So we see that Laura was only two to four years old when they lived in Kansas, and four to seven years old when in Wisconsin the second time. In *Little House in the Big Woods*, the first book in the series, Laura was written as being age four to five, and age six to seven in *Little House on the Prairie.* The memories that Laura wrote of in *Little House in the Big Woods* were mostly from the second time she lived in the big woods, when she was old enough to remember things, plus family stories she heard. *Little House on the Prairie* in Kansas is the second book. Laura did not want to write about living in the big woods for her first two years, then Little House on the Kansas prairie for the next two years, then Little House back in the big woods for four more years. Therefore she simplified the story, as if she had lived in the big woods only one time.

*Little House in the Big Woods* was published in 1932, when Laura was sixty-five years old. So when grown-up Laura wrote about little Laura in the big woods, her hair was grandma gray, her build was pleasantly plump, and the laugh lines around her eyes stayed there, even when she wasn't laughing. All those stories of little brown haired Laura were written by white haired Laura. They were the same person, the same mind, the same heart – the young and old Laura.

Yet at the time that old Laura wrote about the big woods, she was only about two-thirds through her life.

Laura once wrote:

*"Has anyone ever said to you, as a warning, "No man knoweth what a day may bring forth?"*

*I have heard it often and it is always quoted with a melancholy droop at the corners of the mouth.*

*But why?*

*Suppose we do not know what will happen tomorrow. May it not just as well be a happy surprise as something unpleasant?*

*To me it is a joy that "no man knoweth what a day may bring forth" and that life is a journey from one discovery to another."*[4]

When sixty-some-year-old Laura began writing her books, she set out on a great journey of discovery, and that turned out to be a very pleasant and a happy surprise. Her journey forward went backward. She remembered that children called their parents Ma and Pa, instead of Mama and Papa, as her daughter Rose called her and Almanzo, or Mom and Dad, as is common today. She remembered sleeping in a trundle bed that they trundled out from under her parents' bed at night and then trundled back under again in the day, to save space in the small cabin. She remembered hearing wolves howl around her house, and in her mind's eye she could still see them sitting in their yard. Laura remembered Pa hunting in the thick woods for fresh meat, almost as someone later might go to a store. And Laura remembered playing ball with an inflated pig's bladder, hitting it in the air and kicking it along the ground, getting almost as much use out of it as the pig had.

Old Laura wrote that young Laura thought that the big woods of Wisconsin went on as far as a man could walk in a month.

In *Pioneer Girl*, Laura remembered a fire and a man lost in those big woods, soon after the Ingalls returned to the big woods from Kansas.

*"One day the sun was nearly hidden by smoke all day and when dark came the sky was reddened by fire. We stood in the door watching it and soon we could see fire run up to the top of some trees on a hill and then the trees stood there burning like great candles.*

*We heard gunshots off in the woods and Pa said, "Somebody's lost." He took down his rifle and fired it up at the sky several times and after a while a man came to the door. He was a stranger and lost in the woods. Pa told him, if he had gone on the way he was headed, there was nothing but woods between him and the North Pole, whatever that was, but he turned and came in the direction of the shot Pa had fired. It seemed the "Big Woods" as Pa called them were just north of us a ways and they went on and on into the north. I thought our woods were big enough and was going to ask questions about the bigger one when Pa and the strange man went out to fight the fire and Ma put Mary and me to bed in the trundle bed, the little bed that in the daytime was pushed out of the way under the big bed."*

Laura said there were no houses in those big woods, except a few scattered around the edge. There were houses north of them, so the real big woods went on north of that. In fact, Wisconsin was almost all forest – about three-fourths of the state was covered with trees – making nearly a whole state of big woods!

Shortly after the Civil War, about when Laura was born, timbering became a big industry in Wisconsin. By the time Laura and Almanzo moved to Missouri in 1894, Wisconsin was a world leader in lumber production, all from those big woods that went on and on. Sawmills were set up along many of Wisconsin's rivers, logs were floated on those rivers to the sawmills and then cut up into lumber that was shipped east.

After all those trees were cut, part of the big woods became like a big desert. Wherever the trees were clear-cut, the big woods became a big slash pile.

B. E. Fernow was a government forest surveyor. In 1898 he wrote, *"In almost every town in this region, logging has been carried on, and 8,000,000 of the 17,000,000 acres of forest are 'cutover' lands, largely burned-over and waste-brush lands, and one-half of it as nearly desert as it can become in the climate of Wisconsin."*

A history of Wisconsin's forests notes how those 'desert' areas were tinderboxes for forest fires. *"The Cutover led to a variety of problems for contemporary and future residents. Not least among the challenges was the wave of forest fires that cinched the destruction of millions of acres of trees, and took thousands of human lives. Slash (wood residue from logging operations) burned easily and quickly. Fires spread over large areas, leaving ashes in their path."*[5]

We cited how Laura mentioned seeing a fire in the woods near their cabin in the big woods in the fall of 1871. The Ingalls had returned from Kansas that summer, which was a very dry summer in Wisconsin. That autumn, on the other side of the state from the Ingalls, the air was also tinged with smoke from scattered forest fires. The town of Peshtigo, in eastern Wisconsin, lay on both sides of the Peshtigo River, not far from the Green Bay in Lake Michigan. In the 1870 census, the town had 1,749 residents, a fair-sized city for the time, experiencing growth because of the timber surrounding it.

On October 8, a cold front moved in from the west, with stiff, bitter winds. That was not unusual. However, those winds on that day after that dry summer whipped the smaller forest fires up, like a bellows in a blacksmith shop.

Peter Pernin was a minister in the area of Peshtigo, Wisconsin, and he witnessed – and survived – the terrible conflagration that followed those winds. At around 8:30 p.m. that October evening he wrote, *"the menacing crimson reflection on the western sky was rapidly increasing in size and in intensity; in the midst of the unnatural calm and silence reigning around, the strange and terrible noise of fire, strange and unknown thunderous voice of nature."*[6]

Settlers living out in the countryside were caught with nowhere to go as the towering fire quickly leaped from treetop to treetop. Many hurriedly soaked blankets and sought shelter under them in open fields, while men with wet sacks fought the approaching inferno in the shorter grasses. Some did escape with their lives. However, others suffocated as the approaching furnace sucked up all the available oxygen. They avoided the flames, but died when the fire left them no air to breathe.

As the inferno approached the little town of Peshtigo, the pastor described how the terrible winds ran in front of the fire. *"The wind was forerunner of the tempest, increasing in violence, sweeping planks, gate and fencing away into space."*

The wind fanned the flames, but the fire itself created more winds and drafts, fueling it forward until the blaze became so huge that it spawned a tornado – a fire tornado.

The book *Fire at Peshtigo* described how a *"convection column — a whirling chimney of superheated air generated by the fire — suddenly broke through the blanket of heavier, smoke-laden air into the colder air above."* This huge updraft became a fire tornado, a furnace in the forest with incredible heat that made glass out of the sand on the ground. Some survivors stated that the tornado lifted railroad cars and houses, flinging them effortlessly into the air.

The Peshtigo Fire did not spare either part of the divided town, because the huge blaze jumped the river. Amazingly, the wind even carried burning embers across the Green Bay of Lake Michigan, and started new fires on the Door peninsula on the east side of the bay. The entire town of Peshtigo was incinerated. A number of its residents jumped into the river to save themselves, where some died from hypothermia and some drown. Others found safety by climbing down into wells or hunkering in a low marsh. However, many simply did not survive.

After the fire, 1,182 residents of the Peshtigo area were listed as missing. The Peshtigo Fire caused more deaths by fire than any in American history. When the blaze finally burned itself out, an area ten miles by forty miles — well over a million acres — lay scorched and smoking.

When you think of the worst fire in American history, you most likely remember the Great Chicago Fire. After that tragedy, 125 bodies were recovered and estimates were that a total of two to three hundred people died, far fewer than died in the Peshtigo Fire. Yet many have heard of the former; few have heard of the latter.

What's more, the Great Chicago Fire began on the same day as the Peshtigo Fire, that same autumn Sunday evening, October 8, 1871, fanned by the same western winds. Several other Upper Midwest cities suffered major fires that night as well. The Michigan towns of Port Huron, Holland, and Manistee were also destroyed by what is collectively known as the Great Michigan Fire.

Back on Laura's side of the big woods, by the Mississippi River instead of Lake Michigan, the wind also whistled fiercely that night and the cold front brought an October chill to the Ingalls' little gray log cabin. The forest fires there did not rage as badly as they did farther east. The trees on the Ingalls' farm stayed tall and safe. Only later did they learn of the terrible tragedy just east of them. With Mary and Baby Carrie and Ma and Pa all together in the cabin, plus Jack the brindle bulldog curled up in front of the door, Laura was safe in her home at the edge of those big woods, that went on as far as a man could walk in a month.

# Working with Mother

Washing, probably on Monday.
Illustration by Clara E. Atwood
From *A Book of Nursery Rhymes* by Charles Welsh, 1901

*Little House in the Big Woods* says that Ma Ingalls had a weekly routine.

Wash on Monday,
Iron on Tuesday,
Mend on Wednesday,
Churn on Thursday,
Clean on Friday,
Bake on Saturday,
Rest on Sunday.

However, when Laura originally recalled Ma's schedule in *Pioneer Girl*, it was like this.

Wash on Monday,
Iron on Tuesday,
Churn on Wednesday,
Clean on Friday and
Bake on Saturday,

...with mending and sewing and knitting scattered along through the week mixed with the care of the hens and little chickens, working in the garden and feeding the pig. Thursday was unaccounted for in this account, and the churning was moved to Wednesday.

Laura's daughter Rose Wilder Lane recounted the weekly work schedule this way.

*"After the day's routine housework was done, came the week's routine. Only grave sickness or sudden calamity broke that proper routine: washing on Monday, ironing on Tuesday, mending on Wednesday, sewing on Thursday, extra cleaning on Friday, baking on Saturday."*[7]

It seems that although some of the weekly schedules varied, washing was always on Monday. That custom goes back to merry old England, raising doubt as to whether they were really merry on Monday or not. There is an old English nursery rhyme about the weekly work schedule for wives and mothers. The rhyme has a number of versions, varying according to location in England.

Here is the 1854 Northamptonshire version, taken from the *Glossary of Northamptonshire Words and Phrases*.

> *"They that wash on Monday*
> *Have all the week to dry;*
> *They that wash on Tuesday*
> *They have pretty nigh;*
> *They that wash on Wednesday*
> *Have half the week past;*
> *They that wash on Thursday*
> *Are very near the last;*
> *They that wash on Friday*
> *Wash for need;*
> *They that wash on Saturday*
> *Are sluts indeed."*[8]

It seems that the moral of that nursery rhyme is that a wife should do her wash on Monday.

*The Almanack, the Inheritage Journal of History, Travel & Lore*, says that the English custom of washing on Monday migrated to America with some of the first English immigrants.

*"The women of the Mayflower came ashore on Monday, November 13, 1620 (two days after the men). The first thing they did was wash*

*clothing made filthy from sixty-eight days at sea. This established an orderly ritual reflected by the following rhyme:*

> *Wash on Monday,*
> *Iron on Tuesday,*
> *Bake on Wednesday,*
> *Brew on Thursday,*
> *Churn on Friday,*
> *Mend on Saturday,*
> *Go to meeting on Sunday.*"[9]

We can see that this weekly work cycle differs quite a bit from Ma Ingalls's schedule as given in Big Woods. The days for baking, churning and mending are different and Laura does not recall Caroline having a day for brewing at all. But Monday and Tuesday were the same – washing and ironing.

All the way down into the early twentieth century, many women still followed that part of the weekly schedule. Laura wrote an article about a woman who was greatly stressed by the weekly work cycle, even before it began.

*"The feeling of worry and strain caused by trying to carry the whole week's work at once is very tiring. It doesn't pay to be like the woman of years ago in old Vermont, who opened the stairway door at 5 o'clock on Monday morning and called to the hired girl: "Liza! Liza! Hurry up and come down! Today is wash day and the washing not started; tomorrow is ironing day and the ironing not begun; and the next day is Wednesday and here's the week half over and nothing done yet."*[10]

Laura took some steps herself to try to ease that Monday and Tuesday burden.

*"Clothes are so much more sanitary if not ironed after washing,"* *said a physician in an article, on fresh air and sunshine which I read* *the other day. Isn't that delightful news and especially so in hot* *weather? I have not ironed knit underwear, stockings, sheets or* *towels for years but, altho I knew there was a very good reason for* *not doing so, I have always felt rather apologetic about it. Science is* *surely helping the housewife! Now instead of fearing that the* *neighbors will say I am lazy or a poor housekeeper, when they find* *out that I slight my ironing, I can say: "Oh no, I never do much* *ironing, except for the outside clothes. We must not iron out the* *fresh air and sunshine, you know. It is much more healthful not, the* *doctors say." Seriously, there is something very refreshing about* *sheets and pillow slips just fresh from the line, after being washed* *and dried in the sun and air. Just try them that way and see if your* *sleep is not sweeter."*[11]

Going back to the schedule given in Big Woods, of washing, ironing, mending, churning, cleaning and baking – all those jobs were done without the help of machines. The washing was done by boiling and then physically attacking the clothes by either beating or rubbing. Ironing was done with a flat iron heated over the fire. Mending was sewn by hand, churning by the hand and arm, cleaning with rags, mops and brooms, by the hand, arm and back. Baking was on a fireplace or cookstove. Because they had no powered machine helpers, all those jobs took many hours each week, every week, on a certain day of the week.

Laura wrote a humorous article, recalling the time when Almanzo tried to ease the chore of churning for Laura by adding a powered machine, without the power.

"The Man of the Place once bought me a patent churn. "Now," said he, "Throw away that old dash churn. This churn will bring the butter in 3 minutes." It was very kind of him. He had bought the churn to please me and to lighten my work, but I looked upon it with a little suspicion. There was only one handle to turn and opposite it was a place to attach the power from a small engine. We had no engine so the churning must needs be done with one hand, while the other steadied the churn and held it down. It was hard to do, but the butter did come quickly and I would have used it anyway because the Man of the Place had been so kind.

The tin paddles which worked the cream were sharp on the edges and they were attached to the shaft by a screw which was supposed to be loosened to remove the paddles for washing, but I could never loosen it and usually cut my hands on the sharp tin. However, I used the new churn, one hand holding it down to the floor with grim resolution, while the other turned the handle with the strength of despair when the cream thickened. Finally it seemed that I could use it no longer. "I wish you would bring in my old dash churn," I said to the Man of the Place. "I believe it is easier to use than this after all."

"Oh!" said he: "you can churn in 3 minutes with this and the old one takes half a day. Put one end of a board on the churn and the other on a chair and sit on the board, then you can hold the churn down easily!" And so when I churned I sat on a board in the correct mode for horseback riding and tho the churn bucked some I managed to hold my seat. "I wish," said I to the Man of the Place, "you would bring in my old dash churn." (It was where I could not get it.) "I cut my hands on these paddles every time I wash them."

"Oh, pshaw!" said he, "you can churn with this churn in 3 minutes —"

*One day when the churn had been particularly annoying and had cut my hand badly, I took the mechanism of the churn, handle, shaft, wheels and paddles all attached, to the side door which is quite high from the ground and threw it as far as I could. It struck on the handle, rebounded, landed on the paddles, crumpled and lay still and I went out and kicked it before I picked it up. The handle was broken off, the shaft was bent and the paddles were a wreck.*

*"I wish," I remarked casually to the Man of the Place, "that you would bring in my old dash churn. I want to churn this morning."*

*"Oh, use the churn you have," said he. "You can churn in 3 minutes with it. What's the use to spend half a day—"*

*"I can't," I interrupted. "It's broken."*

*"Why how did that happen?" he asked.*

*"I dropped it – just as far as I could," I answered in a small voice and he replied regretfully, "I wish I had known that you did not want to use it, I would like to have the wheels and shaft, but they're ruined now."[12]*

Laura's daughter Rose remembered how much work it was to churn butter in her book *Discovery of Freedom*, released in 1943.

*"Forty years ago, a pound of butter cost an hour's churning in a pottery churn with a wooden splasher, by hand; not to mention all the straining of milk twice a day, and skimming the cream from the pans with a wooden ladle, and washing the strainers and pans and ladle, and running up and down cellar with the cream jar; and this does not mention the chores at the barn.*

*Today the milk flows by thousands of gallons through separators and creameries; machines do the churning and mould the butter and cut* it into quarter-pounds and wrap it in paper and put it into waxed and lithographed boxes; it travels in refrigerated trucks to porcelain electric-refrigerators. And a pound of butter used to cost ten cents and now costs fifty, and actually its cost has been cut in half."[13]

The biggest change in our everyday lives has been the use of powered machines to do our work. Automatic dishwashers wash our dishes. Clothes usually don't need ironing and are so relatively inexpensive that we hardly take the trouble to mend them. Almost no one reading these words has ever churned butter, and those of us who have, did it with an electric mixer. We clean with an electric vacuum cleaner. We bake with an electric or gas oven or a microwave, but few women regularly bake every week, anyway.

What most women in the 1880's spent most of their time doing, women today can do in a fraction of the time, if they do those chores at all. Their life's work is more likely in a corporate factory or office, again greatly assisted by powered machines, whatever that work is.

Yet most women today still too often feel like the lady Laura mentioned: *"Today is wash day and the washing not started; tomorrow is ironing day and the ironing not begun; and the next day is Wednesday and here's the week half over and nothing done yet."* All those machines to help with our chores save us gobs of time, but what happens to all that time?

Laura asked the same question about the motorcar, in an article written in 1917, back when motor cars were just beginning to carry many Americans around.

*"A few days ago, with several others, I attended the meeting of a woman's club in a neighboring town. We went in a motor car,*

*taking less than an hour for the trip on which we used to spend 3 hours, before the days of motor cars, but we did not arrive at the time appointed nor were we the latest comers by any means. Nearly everyone was late and all seemed in a hurry. We hurried to the meeting and were late. We hurried thru the proceedings; we hurried in our friendly exchanges of conversation; we hurried away and we hurried all the way home where we arrived late as usual.*

*What became of the time the motor car saved us? Why was everyone late and in a hurry? I used to drive leisurely over to this town with a team, spend a pleasant afternoon and reach home not much later than I did this time and all with a sense of there being time enough, instead of a feeling of rush and hurry. We have so many machines and so many helps in one way and another, to save time and yet I wonder what we do with the time we save. Nobody seems to have any!*

*Neighbors and friends go less often to spend the day. Instead they say, "We have been planning for so long to come and see you, but we haven't had time," and the answer will be: "Everyone makes the same complaint. People don't go visiting like they used to. There seems to be no time for anything." I have heard this conversation, with only slight variations so many times that I should feel perfectly safe to wager than I should hear it any time the subject might be started. We must have all the time there is the same as always. We should have more, considering the time saving, modern conveniences. What becomes of the time we save?"*[14]

Before we feel too sorry for Ma Ingalls and all the work she had to do compared to our times today, let's take a closer look at their everyday lives in the log cabin in the big woods, without machines.

Each morning, little Laura and Mary helped Ma with the work in the house. They helped clean the dishes and made their own little trundle bed. Then they watched Ma make the butter, remembering how she colored it with a carrot and molded it with a wooden press that left a big strawberry on top of the round of butter. They drank the sour buttermilk left over from the churning after the sweet butter was taken out.

When Ma baked, she gave Laura and Mary a little bit of dough to shape into their own little loaves. When she baked cookies, they got to bake their own little cookies. They watched her carefully, learning without realizing that they were being taught. This was the original homework.

At the end of the day, Caroline and her girls sat down together to relax. Caroline cut out paper dolls from stiff white paper. Those paper dolls did not punch out from a paper doll book, but were carefully drawn and scissored by hand, with each paper doll face being the artwork of Caroline Ingalls. Then Ma took colored paper and cut out delicate little dresses and hats, and even little ribbons and laces. Laura and Mary then dressed their homemade paper dolls with the little paper clothes, designed and manufactured by Caroline's of Wisconsin.

When they did their washing, ironing, mending, churning, cleaning, baking – that work was very important and they all knew it. That work helped make their living on their homestead, their little place on the face of the earth. They planned each day themselves, no one bossed them around, that homestead was their own business, and whether it did well or poorly was their responsibility. They did not want to leave their work to play a game or watch someone else play a game because their work was more important – and more interesting – than a game. Every day their work was important, enriching, and meaningful.

And Caroline and her girls did that work all together.

Many years later, when Laura thought back on the Monday washing, Tuesday ironing, Wednesday mending, Thursday churning, Friday cleaning and Saturday baking – all that work they had done with Ma – this is what she also remembered.

*"The older we grow the more precious become the recollections of childhood's days, especially our memories of mother. Her love and care halo her memory with a brighter radiance, for we have discovered that nowhere else in the world is such loving self sacrifice to be found; her counsels and instructions appeal to us with greater force than when we received them, because our knowledge of the world and our experience of life have proved their worth.*

*The pity of it is that it is by our own experience we have had to gain this knowledge of their value, then when we have learned it in the hard school of life, we know that mother's words were true. So, from generation to generation, the truths of life are taught by precept and generations after generation we each must be burned by fire before we will admit the truth that it will burn.*

*We would be saved some sorry blunders and many a heart ache if we might begin our knowledge where our parents leave off instead of experimenting for ourselves, but life is not that way.*

*Still mother's advice does help and often a word of warning spoken years before will recur to us at just the right moment to save us a misstep. And lessons learned at mother's knee last thru life.*

*But dearer even than mother's teachings are little, personal memories of her, different in each case but essentially the same, mother's face, mother's touch, mother's voice.*"[15]

Laura remembered mother's face, mother's touch, mother's voice – which she had imprinted on her soul from all those days they spent together. When Caroline was making paper dolls, she was also making little girls into moral, upright women.

*"A letter from my mother, who is 76 years old, lies on my desk beside a letter from my daughter, far way in Europe. Reading the message from my mother, I am a child again and a longing unutterable fills my heart for mother's counsel, for the safe haven of her protection and the relief from responsibility which trusting in her judgment always gave me.*

*But when I turn to the letter written by my daughter, who will always be a little girl to me, no matter how old she grows, then I understand and appreciate my mother's position and her feelings toward me.*

*Many of us have the blessed privilege of being at the same time mother and child, able to let the one interpret the other to us until our understanding of both is full and rich. What is there in the attitude of your children toward yourself that you wish were different? Search your heart and learn if your ways toward your own mother could be improved.*

*In the light of experience and the test of the years you can see how your mother might have been more to you, could have guided you better. Then be sure you are making the most of your privileges with the children who are looking to you for guidance. For there is, after all, no great difference between the generations; the problems of today and tomorrow must be met in much the same way as those of yesterday.*

*During the years since my mother was a girl to the time when my daughter is a woman, there have been many slight, external changes, in the fashions and ways of living; some change in the thought of the world and much more freedom in expressing those thoughts. But the love of mother and child is the same, with the responsibility of controlling and guiding on the one side and the obligation of obedience and respect on the other.*

*The most universal sentiment in the world is that of mother love. From the highest to the lowest in the scale of humanity and all thru the animal kingdom it is the strongest force in creation, the conserver of life, the safeguard of evolution. It holds within its sheltering care the fulfillment of the purpose of creation itself. In all ages, in all countries it is the same, a boundless, all enveloping love; if necessary a sacrifice of self for the offspring.*

*Think of the number of children in the world, each the joy of some mother's heart, each a link connecting one generation with another, each a hope for the future. There are more than 20 million school children in the United States; they would fill four cities the size of New York or eight the size of Chicago. We are told that if placed in an unbroken line four abreast, they would reach across the continent from San Francisco to the city of Washington, and there still would be several thousand children waiting to get into line.*

*It stuns the mind to contemplate their numbers and their possibilities, for these are the coming rulers of the world, the makers of destiny, not only for their own generations but for the generations to come. And they are being trained for their part in the procession of time by the women of today. Surely, "The hand that rocks the cradle is the hand that rules the world."*[16]

Long after the paper dolls were torn up and thrown away, the products produced by Caroline's of Wisconsin continued.

*"Mother passed away this morning" was the message that came over the wires and a darkness overshadowed the spring sunshine; a sadness crept into the birds songs.*

*Some of us have received such messages. Those who have not, one day will. Just as when a child, home was lonely when mother was gone, so to children of a larger growth, the world seems a lonesome place when mother has passed away and only memories of her are left us, happy memories if we have not given ourselves any cause for regret.*

*Memories! We go thru life collecting them whether we will or not! Sometimes I wonder if they are our treasures in heaven or the consuming fires of torment when we carry them with us as we, too, pass on.*

*What a joy our memories may be or what a sorrow! But glad or sad they are with us forever. Let us make them carefully of all good things, rejoicing in the wonderful truth that while we are laying up for ourselves the very sweetest and best of happy memories, we are at the same time giving them to others."*[17]

When Laura wrote about Pa in her articles, she wrote about what he did. When Laura wrote about Ma in her articles, she wrote about mother love.

Happy memories – sitting by the fire on a snowy Wisconsin evening, Ma mending, Pa fiddling, the fire flickering an orange glow on the hearth and the kerosene lamp sending a warm yellow light out the window onto the falling flakes. There was a steadiness and security in knowing that Monday was for washing, Tuesday was for ironing, and nights were for sitting around the fire with those you loved, and those who loved you and always would love you.

# Telling Stories by the Fire

Fireplace Waiting for a Family.

In the winter evenings, Laura watched Pa clean his musket rifle, but it was the stories that came afterward that really fired up her memory.

Today many people think that only criminals and governments should have guns. In Pa Ingalls' time, practically every man on the frontier had a gun, yet there were few criminals.

Laura mentioned that Pa had to hit a bear or a panther with his first shot, because it took him so long to reload his gun. There were different types of musket rifles, each with its own loading time.

One type that was widely used in the Civil War could be reloaded fairly quickly, getting off perhaps three shots per minute.[18] The round ball that the musket shot was simply dropped down into the barrel, because it didn't fit so tightly. Since it didn't fit tightly, its accuracy and range were lessened when it was blasted out.

The type of musket that Pa had, though, was more accurate. The bullet fit tightly into the barrel, giving it more range and accuracy, but each bullet had to be pounded down into the barrel. That pounding process used up a lot of time, so it took Pa about three minutes to reload and get another shot off.

Meaning –

If Pa shot at a bear and didn't finish him off, that could make for an interesting three minutes. Surely Pa's heart would be pounding while he was pounding another bullet into the rifle barrel. A bear can run a *long* way in three minutes.

At night in the cabin, after Pa had cleaned his rifle and made bullets for the next day's hunting, he told his girls stories. Those were not just made-up stories or figments of a fertile imagination. They were real life sagas, tales that he had heard from his folks and tales that he and Ma had lived.

What's the difference between a real story and a made-up story? Everything. One is real. One is not.

In 1937, after several of her books had been published and acclaimed, Laura mentioned Pa's stories in a speech.

*"In Detroit Laura gave a speech at the Children's Book Fair on why she wrote her books. "We had a busy, happy childhood," she said, "but of it all, sister Mary and I loved Pa's stories best. We never forgot them, and I have always felt they were too good to be altogether lost. Children today could not have a childhood like mine in the Big Woods of Wisconsin, but they could learn from it and hear the stories that Pa used to tell."*[19]

*Little House in the Big Woods* has a less developed plot than her other books, and is mostly a reciting of how the Ingalls did their everyday work and of Pa's stories. A big part of Laura's motivation for writing her books was to preserve the family stories that Pa told on those winter evenings. In *Little House in the Big Woods*, she succeeded.

In chapter 1, Laura began with the story of Pa seeing a bear by their pigpen. He shot at the bear and missed. The bear then ran away, instead of trying to get Pa while he was reloading. Although he regretted missing the bear, Pa did save the pig, and his dry comment was, *"Anyway, I saved the bacon."*

In chapter 2, Pa came upon a bear in the woods that had caught and killed a pig. Pa killed the bear and brought both it and the pig home. His wry comment there was, *"So I just brought home the bacon."*

Apparently, Pa was really big on bacon.

It doesn't take much imagination to see little Laura and Mary asking Pa to tell them those stories over and over. Then, at the end of his yarns about the bears and the pigs, Pa would say, with a terrific twinkle in his bright blue eyes, "I saved the bacon," or "I just brought home the bacon." Each time those statements were surely met with squeals of laughter. Laura told the pig stories in a narrative form, yet she thought so much of Pa's bacon barbs that she quoted them directly.

Maybe Laura was big on bacon, too.

Also in chapter two, Laura told the story of "Grandpa and the Panther." This story and several others even have a separate title in the book to set the story off within the chapter. The tale may have grown a little through the years, as Grandpa told it and then Pa retold it, but the net result was that after hearing the story, Laura and Mary snuggled up close to Pa and felt safe and protected from all panthers.

The third chapter includes the story of Pa and the screech owl, also set apart with a separate title, when Pa was a naughty little boy and did not bring the cows directly home. Again, we can almost hear the giggles of laughter when Pa concluded that he had been scared by only a screech owl.

The fourth chapter includes a story not set off by itself, but told in dialogue. Pa's older brother Peter and Ma's younger sister Eliza and family came for a Christmas visit. The youngsters, double first cousins, listened as the adults talked by the fire, when Eliza and Peter recounted how their dog Prince had saved Eliza from a panther attack by not letting her go outside. That was not one of Pa's stories, but he likely repeated it a time or two for his girls, on a snowed-in winter's evening, to show the value of a good dog. Jack the brindle bulldog probably liked that story.

Chapter five includes the story of Grandpa's sled and the passenger pig, again set off with a title. Grandpa and his brothers built a sled but hadn't tried it out before Sunday came. When their father fell asleep on Sunday afternoon, they sneaked out for just one sled run, only to pick up a squealing pig on the way. Don't you know that every time Pa told the story of the pig squealing on top of the boys on the sled, there was a lot more squealing going on around the fire in the Ingalls cabin?

The sixth chapter tells two stories about bears. The first story is not set off as a story but is part of the plot of the chapter. In the dark, Ma mistook a bear for Sukey their cow and slapped him to get him to move. Over the following years, the family surely retold and discussed the story of Sukey the Bear.

The other bear story is set off with the title "The Story of Pa and the Bear in the Way." That was when Pa was stumped by a bear that turned out to be a stump.

Did you notice that those two stories, about Sukey Bear and Stumpy Bear, and several other family stories, were about encounters with wild animals? Such was everyday life on the frontier.

We find the same thing in chapter ten. Pa and a bear both found a honey bee tree. Pa ran the bear off and then made off with the honey. Modern beekeepers wear all sorts of protective garb to keep from getting stung and one of the unexplained twists in this story is why the bees never stung Pa.

When the Ingalls enjoyed family stories by the fireplace, they were not alone, at that period in America. Winter nights were too long to sleep all the way through, darkness came early, the houses were cold, so in the winter everyone – the entire family – gathered around the hearth, just as people gather around a campfire on a cool evening. Family tales were told and retold. There were no electronic gadgets to steal time and attention away from the family. Reading was an enjoyable family activity, where one member read for the rest, but books were at a premium and family libraries hardly deserved the title. Music was a family activity where all could join in either playing an instrument or singing, but not for hours on end. Games like checkers were played, with some skill. A main activity of a family, though, was just talking with each other, which meant that family stories got repeated and relearned.

Lest we think that such evenings were insufferably boring, a *Wall Street Journal* article brought up the positive effect of family stories on younger members of the family.

*"An Emory University study of 65 families with children ages 14 to 16 found kids' ability to retell parents' stories was linked to a lower rate of depression and anxiety and less acting-out of frustration or anger, says Robyn Fivush, a psychology professor. Knowing family stories "helps children put their own experience in perspective," Dr. Fivush says."*

The article then gave a personal example of that positive effect.

*"When C. Stephen Guyer's three children were growing up, he told them stories about how his grandfather, a banker, lost all in the 1930s, but didn't lose sight of what he valued most. In one of the darkest times, Mr. Guyer says, when his grandfather was nearly broke, he loaded his family into the car and took them to see family members in Canada. The message: "There are more important things in life than money," says Mr. Guyer, of Littleton, Colo.*

*The tale took on new relevance recently, when Mr. Guyer downsized to a small house from a more luxurious one. He was worried that his children, a daughter, 15, and twins, 22, would be upset. To his surprise, they weren't. Instead, their reaction echoed their great-grandfather's. "What they care about," Mr. Guyer says his children told him, "is how warm are the people in the house, how much of their heart is accessible.""*

Piercing questions for any family –

How warm are the people in the house?

How much of their heart is accessible?

Somehow, televisions, particularly with modern program-ming, do not lend themselves to family warmth and communication. In fact, communication between family members is hindered because watching TV and videos requires halting most communication. Web surfing, video games, and audio players all inherently block close communication between people and encourage cocooning. Today many families, even if they are in the same house together at night, are still very much by themselves in spirit, with each member more engaged with an electronic device than with anyone else in the family. Often, even while a family is together, they are isolated from each other.

How different it was then! And 'then' was the whole period of human history before the middle of the twentieth century.

Can you see what it was like in the Ingalls' log cabin, in the big Wisconsin woods, when Laura was a little girl?

Log cabins were usually built one log long and one log wide, perhaps twenty feet by sixteen feet. A sleeping attic gave more room, but that was only for sleeping, not for moving around because it was, after all, just an attic. The Ingalls cabin had a small bedroom walled off on one end. Their one main room was like their living room or great room, but that was also practically the whole house. The great room had two windows, both with glass. The small bedroom had a window, too, but no glass, only a wooden shutter. Usually cabins had only one door, but Pa's cabin had a door in front and in back. The floor was usually split logs that didn't fit perfectly together. There was very little furniture, just a table and chairs and a cookstove. The dishes sat on shelves – that was the cup board, the board where you set the cups. A big stone fireplace took up one end of the cabin. That was at the center of the great room, the focal point of the house and the gathering spot for the family.

You might think of it as their big screen TV.

By the time supper was finished, the somber darkness of winter surrounded the little log house in the deep woods that sat all alone, short and squat amidst the tall, towering trees. Only a faint, dim light in the window of the cabin broke the darkness of those woods, as the oil lamp vainly tried to light up the forest. After supper, the dishes were cleaned and the dishwater was dumped far enough behind the house to avoid looking untidy in the snow that hardly melted before spring.

Then, whatever they were doing, they all gathered at the hearth, the heart of the home. The dictionary even equates hearth with home: *"hearth - home symbolized as a part of the fireplace; "driven from hearth and home.""*

Around the hearth, Ma mended, Pa made bullets, baby Carrie slept and Laura and Mary played paper dolls by the fire. After a while, Pa hung his gun over the door, Ma laid her mending back in its bottomless basket, and the girls carefully stored their paper dolls away. Ma turned off the oil lamp, to save on the costly oil. No light at all came in the window, which only showed that it was a window by firelight reflecting off the black shiny panes. With all light gone, they turned to the only light in that part of the whole forest – their fireplace.

Firelight always flickers. It is always described as flickering, and indeed that's what it always does. The light is not steady and straight, but always moving and changing, brightening up, dimming down, flitting around. Laura and Mary sat on the floor by the hearth; Ma and Pa sat in their chairs on either side of the fire. Behind them, the red and yellow glow lit up the log walls, making a shadow for each of the four Ingalls. Their shadows did not move, but around those black silhouettes the firelight danced all over the rounded logs, the light always there but always darting here and there.

The trees, the snow and the weighty winter cold killed all sound around the house. Even the wind was whipped and submitted meekly to the chill. The silence slid into the darkness, and they two became one, in the cold, dark, still night.

Except by the fireplace. The fire sent out little noises that seemed big, because they were the only noises to be heard.

The logs popped, sometimes sizzled, as the fire continually ate into its stacked loading. The logs were piled high, the fire was necessarily big, and the pops and crackles and sizzles and whistles were frequent and steady. That was the only noise in the cabin. There were no hums and no whirs, from inside or outside, nowhere was there sound to be found, except for the little sounds that seemed big, coming from the fire. The fire in the fireplace was the only thing that was going on in that whole section of the woods.

Pa sat there with his roughish beard and thick tousled hair, across from Ma with her demure smile that was always almost ready to break out on her face. Laura and Mary sat, hardly wiggling at all, as the end of the day began to weigh on them. All there together in the little log cabin in the big, deep woods, sitting in the shadows and making shadows, they all stared at the fire, as they always did, with its hypnotic glow, being soothed and warmed and calmed.

Out of the silence, one of the girls asked Pa to tell them a story. A small smile crossed his lips and his voice slowly rolled out. The two young ones shifted their eyes back and forth between their father and the fire. Caroline listened, too; the stories were really for their girls, but she followed the familiar words from the familiar voice, and added bits of detail here and there. As he told the story, Pa's voice was not loud – Carrie was asleep – but it was easily heard. His hands didn't move much, but his eyes did, lighting up his tale with darts of excitement and twinkles of tension.

Then he finished, right where everyone expected, with the ending that everyone knew was coming.

*"Anyway, I saved the bacon."*

After the squeals of laughter died down, he rose to stir the fire, but he had already stirred the souls of his little daughters. Laura made a whole book, or even several books, out of those family stories. It turns out, after all, that Laura helped Pa save the bacon.

When Laura heard those stories around that fire, though, she learned more than family history. She learned family values. Laura not only absorbed the family tales. She absorbed the pioneer character that they showed. An article in *National Affairs* titled "Lessons in Liberty" points to that character.

*"Wilder's decision to chronicle her family's travels was clearly driven by a sense of admiration for what her parents, and their fellow pioneers, had accomplished. Chief among those accomplishments was their kindling of "the spirit of the frontier," which Wilder believed her mother and father had "possessed...to a marked degree." But Wilder was also motivated by the sense that, at the time when she was writing her books — during the Great Depression and the New Deal — that spirit seemed to be fading away.*

*At the heart of that deteriorating ethic was self-reliance; it was that virtue, above all, that Wilder intended to communicate in her fictional books..."*

*"But the relevant point for using Wilder's books as a basis for cultural and historical rediscovery is less the strict facts of her biography and more the moral of her stories. To that end, it is worth noting that, in Wilder's effort to produce, as she put it, a "true picture of the times and the place and the people," it was the virtue of independence that she wanted her readers to understand and remember above all. Indeed, as Wilder stated in the Sorosis Club speech, "Running through all the stories, like a golden thread, is the*

*same thought of the values of life. They were courage, self reliance, independence, integrity and helpfulness."* To Wilder, *these values defined the pioneer experience."*[20]

Pa's family stories carried the history of the family, but they also carried the character of the family, and like a golden thread, those unchanging values of life came through to us in Laura's books.

# iGifts

*Woman Sewing*, making something by hand.
From a 1898 charcoal drawing by D. A. C. Artz

When a gift is made by a machine, it is precisely produced, just like thousands of others on that production line.

When a gift is made by someone you love, it's a work of art.

In chapter four, titled "Christmas," Pa spent some of his evening hours by the fire with three boards, in two different sizes.

Put yourself in his place. You have three boards.

Now what?

Could you make a beautiful gift out of those?

Pa could.

He sanded and polished the boards, sanding them with sandpaper but polishing them with his hand. That gives further meaning to the phrase hand-polished.

Then he whittled on the edges of the polished boards. He did that with his jackknife, which is a pocketknife with a blade that folds into the knife so it can be carried in a pocket. Knives originally did not fold, which made carrying them in a pocket somewhat uncomfortable. Sometimes people say that a truck jackknifes, when its trailer folds up toward the cab, the way a jackknife folds.

Pa's jackknife was very sharp. Pioneers took good care of their tools, and a cutting tool, like an axe, scythe, or knife, must be kept sharp to cut well. Abraham Lincoln said that if he had six hours to cut down a tree, he would spend four hours sharpening his axe.[21] Pioneers kept their cutting tools sharp.

Pa used his sharp knife to whittle the wood, or cut designs in the wood. Men used to whittle to while away the time, if they had the time to while away. Sometimes when men would sit and visit, they would whittle while they talked, if they weren't too involved in the talking. Some became good whittlers, since they had extensive practice, and whittling became a country art. Many men also became good talkers, for the same reason.

Pa cut stars, circles, curlicues, leaves, and birds on the edges of the boards. He carefully planned each little cutting, then painstakingly cut out the wood in the shape that he wanted, leaving a tiny bird or leaf or star or circle. All of those carvings took a lot of time, Pa's time, with Pa's hands. When he finished, Pa had a gift for Caroline, a hand polished, hand carved shelf to hold Ma's china shepherdess.

Pioneers were very practical. They had to be, to stay alive. They couldn't even spare enough time to make spare time. Yet Charles went to all that trouble, on all those winter evenings in the dim cabin, after hunting all day, doing chores that evening, and making bullets that night – he spent his precious time carving and cutting, sanding and polishing, making his gift for Caroline.

Did that shelf feed Caroline? Did it keep her warm? Did it keep the bears away when she went to milk the cow?

No.

Then what did that little shelf do?

That shelf showed Charles' love for Caroline.

Every time she walked by it.

How many times, in her busy, busy days, did Ma pause for a brief moment in front of that shelf, and take a minute to examine the leaves and birds, all cut carefully and delicately by hand?

Charles' hand.

Those birds and leaves told her that Charles loved her. He had taken all that time, his time, his trouble, his care to make her special shelf, only because he loved her enough to do that.

*Oh, Charles!*

That year, Laura received a gift of a pair of mittens and a piece of peppermint candy. Mittens are a practical gift. They kept Laura's hands warm in the winter, but more than that, those mittens were made by Ma's hands, knitted by the firelight when Ma was finished with her day's work. So when Laura wore her mittens on her hands, she remembered Ma's hands.

Pa and Uncle Peter and the cousins also received mittens, all made by hand. Eliza gave Caroline an apple spiced with cloves, and Caroline gave Eliza a little book to hold needles, again homemade and handmade.

The gift that Laura loved most of all was her rag doll. A rag doll is made out of rags. Rags were what was left from used clothing, clothes that had been worn so long they absolutely couldn't be worn any longer.

They were real, honest to goodness rags.

Rags were not thrown away. They were used to make quilts, for patches on other clothing, and for little girls' rag dolls. Rags were an early form of recycling.

In her book *Old Home Town*, Rose Wilder Lane remembered the rags that her mother and grandmother had saved, although the names were changed in the book.

*"Every house had a scrap-bag and every scrap of cloth was treasured. Nothing was more pleasant than sitting down, in the satisfaction of knowing that all the work was done, to spread out those bits of cloth, lay the pattern on them at various angles to determine how to cut without waste, and then with sharp shears to cut out the squares and triangles. Women looked forward to this for days, saying, "As soon as I get this job out of the way, I'm going to get at the scrap-bag!" They said to neighbors, "What are you doing tomorrow afternoon? Bring over your scrap-bag and let's just spend the whole afternoon cutting out quilt patches."*

*Scrap-bags were always interesting. "My, isn't that the Turkey red that Ethel wore that time she recited, 'Curfew Shall Not Ring Tonight'?" Yes, and how cute she was. And this is the last of that dress that grandma hated so, but wore every summer because grandfather bought the goods to surprise her. "She never could bear plaids." And here was the pink-and-white check Susan wore the summer before she was married. "I wore this sage green with the chocolate stripes when I was a girl. It's kind of old-fashioned now, but John always admired it." And, "My land, I thought the last of this was in the bedroom carpet! The dress I wore to Fourth of July, that time the horses ran away.""*[22]

And from such a scrap-bag was born Laura's rag doll.

A rag doll is not finely detailed, and doesn't have eyes that open and shut nor a finely shaped mouth. Rags cannot be shaped that way. With Laura's rag doll, a bit of white rag made her face, onto which two black buttons were sewn for eyes, over which two pencil lines were drawn for eyebrows. Her cheeks and lips were pokeberry stain. Pokeberries look delicious, but are poison to eat. They are deep purple, and when squished will stain whatever they touch with a scarlet stain, as on the white cloth that was the doll's face, for cheeks and lips. The doll's hair was strings of yarn. The yarn was probably from an old sweater, then the knitting was raveled or unraveled, with both words meaning the same thing. When the yarn came loose, it was curly, and that made the doll's hair curly.

So Laura's doll was just rags, truly a rag doll. But Ma had gone to a lot of trouble with those rags. The rag doll had tiny stockings made of colorful red flannel, which showed up quite well with the tiny black cloth shoes, although the doll didn't really have feet and her hands were just thread stitched onto the cloth to look like fingers. Ma even made little gaiters, which go over the tops of the shoes to keep out the snow. The doll also had a lovely pink and blue calico dress made just for her, so that although just a rag doll, she was still somewhat stylish.

Mary already had a rag doll, and with Ma's gift, Laura had one of her own. She loved those sewn rags so well that she gave it a name – Charlotte, the same name as Laura's grandmother, Caroline's mother. Later, when the Ingalls lived on Plum Creek, a neighbor girl took Laura's doll home with her. Afterward Laura found Charlotte tossed in a mud hole, with her hair pulled off and one button eye pulled out. Laura took Charlotte home to Ma, where Ma cleaned her up, and with some more rags, made her as good as new again, albeit with a slightly different look.

When Laura got married, she packed her things in a box to take to Almanzo's house. The first thing she put in the box was Charlotte, the rag doll from the big woods.

To repeat for emphasis: The first thing Laura put in the box that began the rest of her life was Charlotte, the rag doll from the big woods.

Every time that she held Charlotte, or when she plucked Charlotte out of the neighbor's mud hole and sneaked her back home, or when she carefully packed Charlotte in the bottom of her box to take to her new home, what did Laura see in that bit of rags?

Laura saw Caroline's love. She loved Charlotte, but through that pokeberry stained doll with yarn hair, that Ma had carefully cut and sewed and then re-sewed, Laura saw her mother's love for her.

Today young people receive gifts of iPods, iPads and iPhones. They seldom receive iGifts.

Have you ever had a gift that was made by the hands of someone who loved you, a gift that was made just for you, and no one else in the whole world had a gift just like the one that was made just for you, because it was made just for you?

That is an iGift, a gift that I took the time, trouble and care to make just for you, because I love you. An iGift like Pa made for Caroline or like Caroline made for her girls is a gift that is low tech and high love.

When a gift is made by a machine, it is precisely produced, like thousands of others on that production line. Factory made gifts look perfect, but they're not. Factory made gifts made by machines are never made with love. Machines don't have hands, souls or hearts. People do.

When a gift is made by someone beloved, it's a work of art.

No.

It's more than that.

When a gift is made by someone beloved, it's a work of heart.

An iGift.

# Saturday Night Bath, Needed or Not

It's that time of the week.
Illustration by Clara E. Atwood
From *A Book of Nursery Rhymes*, by Charles Welsh, 1901

The Saturday night bath was a big splash.

Really.

In both of her first two books, Laura included a detailed description of the Saturday night bath. Laura may have included that weekly ritual because she knew it was passing. Not that people stopped bathing; they just began to bathe more often. Daughter Rose built Laura and Almanzo a new house in 1928, which had all the modern conveniences. So when Laura wrote of the Saturday night bath, for her that was just a memory of the way things used to be.

In *Little House in the Big Woods*, the Saturday night bath was included in the "Sunday" chapter. Laura described how the girls and Ma and Pa got their weekly scrubbing in a washtub in the kitchen on Saturday night.

In *Farmer Boy*, Laura wrote of Almanzo gathering icicles from the roof into the washtub, then melting them on the stove. He dipped hot water from the tub on the stove into another tub on the floor. Then he bathed in that tub in front of the stove's open oven door, to keep warm. Actually, the half that was facing the oven was too hot, and the half that was facing the other way was too cold. So, in the wintertime at least, Almanzo did not luxuriate in a long, hot bath. He bathed quickly, while rotating his body to keep the hot part cool and the cool part warm, which must have been very difficult to do in a small, round washtub. After his bath, his mother gave him an elbow to ear inspection, and if he was squeaky clean, he was sent off to bed. On Saturday night, he felt good being clean; that may give an indication of how he felt on Friday night. But he did not enjoy that Saturday night clean feeling enough to make him want to bathe each week. He would rather have bathed only in the spring.

That was a schedule which some in olden times apparently followed, as part of the annual spring cleaning.

In the Wilder family as told in *Farmer Boy*, the youngest bathed first, followed by the next oldest, and then all the way through Mother and Father Wilder. In the big woods in Wisconsin in wintertime, Pa Ingalls scooped up a heaping tub of snow that melted into a few inches of heated bath water. They, too, bathed the youngest first and the oldest last. The water was thrown out after each bather and new hot water added for the next. Historically, that order was often reversed. The oldest bathed first, other family members followed in age order, with the youngest baby getting bathed last. They all used the same bath water, with the dirty water being thrown out after the little baby's bath. Some say that the saying, "Don't throw the baby out with the bath water" stems from this custom.[23] That's originally a German proverb from at least half a millennia ago so its origin is murky, but it seems reasonable that the saying may have come from murky water.

How could people of long ago have been so casual about their cleanliness?

They had no real choice. Bathing, especially in winter, took a lot of work and time. Most people worked dawn to dusk just to get enough food to stay alive. Clean elbows and ears ranked way below growling stomachs in importance.

Before you put up too much of a stink over the way they must have, consider how much work went into a wintertime bath.

All the bath water had to be lugged up from the spring or well. In the far north, like the Ingalls in Wisconsin or the Wilders in New York State, they could simply step out the door and gather snow or icicles. On the other hand, when they went outside to get that snow or ice, that might have iced their desire to bathe.

Icy water doesn't heat up quickly. A watched pot never boils; neither does a watched washtub. The fire had to be stoked and re-stoked to keep the heating going, taking extra wood or coal just for that night's bathing. While the bathing was going on, no one else could go into the bathing area.

In short, the family worked the whole night until bedtime – lugging water, heating water, stoking the stove, bringing in more wood, throwing out the water – just to get everyone a bath.

Was Almanzo right in wanting to bathe only in the spring?

That might depend on which way the wind was blowing, as one opinion has it.

*"One would have been well advised to stand upwind of anyone one was having a conversation with in the 19th century. The only parts of the body that were at all frequently washed were the arms, neck, face, and hands. However, by the mid-19th century, house plans show that houses had begun to install special houses for baths. In the middle class usually the whole family took part in one big bath on Saturday, mostly because of the nuisance it was to boil the water. The poor, however, bathed infrequently at best."*[24]

Shakespeare's Juliet told Romeo that a rose by any other name would smell just as sweet. Remember, though, that she spent much of her time way up in the balcony.[25]

Queen Elizabeth may have smelled a bit sweeter than most.

*"[I]n England, Elizabeth I, after whom Virginia was named, found a bath befitting to a virgin queen and took to it once a month "whether she need it or no." "*[26]

Indeed, bathing was sometimes thought unbecoming for a lady.

*"In her treatise for French women, <u>On Politeness and Good Taste, or the Duties of a Christian Woman in the World,</u> published in 1860, the Countess Drohojowska advised: "Never take more than one bath a month. There is in the taste for sitting down in a bathtub a certain indolence and softness that ill suits a woman." The Countess de Pange recalled, "No-one in my family took a bath!" They washed in a tub filled with two inches of water or sponged themselves, rather than sinking into water up to their necks, which seemed "pagan, even sinful."*[27]

One Quaker woman hadn't been wet all over at once for twenty-eight years. Her skin must have been shocked when it was finally submerged, but she bore it better than expected.

*"Among early American settlers, William Penn's Quakers espoused healthy habits of exercise and hygiene. Told that vigorous activity for children "fits them to bear the roughest Providences," Quakers quickly took to swimming and bathing. One, Elizabeth Drinker, had a shower put up, tried it, and noted, "I bore it better than I expected, not having been wett [sic] all over at once, for 28 years past.""*[28]

Amazingly, this pattern of infrequent bathing prevailed through much of human history, until less than a century ago. It was just too much work to bathe more often. In many parts of the world, infrequent bathing is still a normal way of life.

However, more fastidious folks did have ways to cope with their lack of indoor plumbing. Homes had a pitcher and washbasin, considered decorative objects now, but originally used for daily washing.

The *Old Farmer's Almanac* had a suggestion for common hygiene in Victorian times.

*"Upon arising, take a complete bath. A simple washing out of the eyes is not sufficient. The complete bathing of the body once each day is of the utmost importance. Not more than a quart of water is necessary, preferably rainwater."*[29]

Bathing in a quart of water required far less work than bathing in a whole tub of water. A person simply washed himself with a rag. Of course, scrubbing with a wet rag is not as cleansing as soaking in a tub or dousing in a shower, but it will serve to keep the body fairly clean.

*The Household Cyclopedia of General Information* listed these rules for living in 1881.

*"1. Rise early, and never sit up late.*

*2. Wash the whole body every morning with cold water, by means of a large sponge, and rub it dry with a rough towel, or scrub the whole body for ten or fifteen minutes with flesh brushes.*

*3. Drink water generally, and avoid excess of spirits, wine, and fermented liquors.*

*4. Keep the body open by the free use of the syringe, and remove superior obstructions by aperient pills."*

Washing every morning with cold water was efficient in use of time, because no water had to be heated at all. However, houses often were not well heated in winter, and the idea of washing all over with cold water on a cold winter morning in a chilly, drafty house was probably not followed by too many people, as John Quincy Adams' grandson noted.

*"Up in New England, winter washing was a severe trial, and bathing was unthinkable. "When the temperature of a bed-room*

ranges below the freezing-point, there is no inducement ... to waste any unnecessary time in washing," wrote Charles Francis Adams, grandson of President John Quincy Adams and brother of historian Henry Adams."[30]

The cyclopedia's other guidelines about going to bed and rising early and drinking a lot of water sound good enough, but that one about keeping the body open by free use of the syringe and removing superior obstructions by aperient pills definitely sounds unappealing.

Mary Ingalls went to the School for the Blind in Vinton, Iowa. That institution had these guidelines about cleanliness.

*"Most students' rooms were furnished with two beds with two students assigned to each bed. The beds had "wire bottoms" (springs) with mattresses stuffed with either wool or husks. Bed linen was usually changed weekly. Older students were allowed to choose their bed partners. They were also required to care for their living quarters with matrons assisting whenever help and guidance were needed.*

*All students were required to change their clothes once a week and take a bath each Saturday. A half-hour period was assigned to each individual for that purpose. Teachers supervised and assisted with the bathing of younger children or even with any older students who were careless in carrying out the bathing requirements."*[31]

Since she was raised in a proper manner for the times, we assume that Mary had no trouble changing her clothes every week and bathing every Saturday night.

Rose's novel *Diverging Roads* was somewhat autobiographical. Helen, the heroine of the book, marveled at a bathtub, far superior to the old washtub.

*"The room rented for six dollars a month. It had a large bow-window overlooking the street, gaily flowered wall-paper, a red carpet, a big wooden bed, a wash-stand with pitcher and bowl, and two rocking chairs. At the end of the long hall was a bathroom with a white tub in it, the first Helen had seen. There was something metropolitan about that tub; a bath in it would be an event far different from the Saturday night scrubs in the tin wash-tub at home."*

In a 1916 article, Laura poked a little fun at the Saturday night bath, which custom they probably still followed at the time.

*"Some time ago the semi-annual house-cleaning was dropped from my program, very much to everyone's advantage. If a room needed cleaning out of season, I used to think "Oh well, it will soon be house-cleaning time" and let it wait until then. I found that I was becoming like the man who did "wish Saturday would come so that he could take a bath.""*[32]

Rose remembered their Saturday night baths and clean Sundays in her book *Old Home Town*, about her home town of Mansfield, Missouri.

*"We woke clean from the previous night's bath; fresh underwear felt strange against the skin; by nine o'clock we were getting into Sunday clothes. Men and boys looked unfamiliar in their best suits with boiled shirts and stiff collars, knotted four-in-hands and polished shoes. The church bells rang a sweeter but no less imperative summons than the school bell, accelerating the last-minute scurry of thrusting in hat-pins, tying veils not unbearably tight over the nose, pinning the watch to the bosom and smoothing black kid down compressed fingers. Petticoats rustled feverishly and voices grew sharp. "Have you a handkerchief? Did you put out the cat? Have you locked the back door, are you sure?" "Hurry, we'll be*

late." "Well, it's not my fault if we are, I was ready –" "Oh, my goodness, don't just stand there talking!" Then the key turned in the front door, and decorum encased us."[33]

In that same book, Rose tells of a neighbor who really, really got tired of heating the Saturday night bath water.

"Mrs. Sherwood said the thing that she minded most of all was the bath-water.

"I'll be married twenty-five years next Thanksgiving," Mrs. Sherwood said. "And every single Saturday night for twenty-four years and eight months and three weeks I've dipped water out of the rain-water barrel, and strained it, and lugged the washtub into the kitchen to set on the supper fire to heat for Mr. Sherwood's bath. And put out the washrag and towel and soap for him, and laid out his clean underwear and his socks. And seems to me sometimes I'll scream. Seems to me I can't do it one single Saturday more. I been sitting here thinking and I ought to go do it and seems to me I just can't. Nobody'd want a better husband or a kinder. But if only once he'd get his own bath-water ready. Or not take a bath. Even not take a bath. Just anything different. I'm an old woman now and no use looking forward to anything any more but seems to me I could stand it all if only it wasn't for Saturdays and the bath-water."[34]

It seems that Mrs. Sherwood tended to agree with Almanzo, that a springtime bath was best.

At about the time that Laura began writing her books, the country began changing its custom of bathing on Saturday night. As we said, that may well be the reason that Laura included a detailed description of the ritual.

Jules Verne was the author of the famous science fiction novels *Journey to the Center of the Earth, Twenty Thousand Leagues Under the Sea,* and *Around the World in Eighty Days.* In his short story "Day in the Life of an American Journalist in 2889," written in 1889, he wrote about the bath of the future.

*"There is always a bath prepared in the hotel, and I do not even have to bother to leave my room in order to take it. If I just press this switch the bath will start moving, and you will see it appear all by itself with water at a temperature of 37C." Francis pressed the switch. There was a muffled noise which swelled in volume... Then one of the doors opened and the bath appeared, sliding on its rails."[35]*

Verne is considered somewhat prescient in his science fiction predictions. However, we have gone far beyond having a bath slide into the room on rails and we're nowhere near 2889. How did we go from bathing on Saturday night to having a shower every day?

*The Mainspring of Human Progress*, a book by Henry Grady Weaver published in 1947, gives this reason.

*"Why did men die of starvation for 6,000 years? Why is it that we in America have never had a famine?*

*Why did men walk and carry goods (and other men) on their straining backs for 6,000 years - then suddenly, on only a small part of the earth's surface, the forces of nature are harnessed to do the bidding of the humblest citizen?*

*Why did families live for 6,000 years in caves and floorless hovels, without windows or chimneys - then within a few generations, we in America take floors, rugs, chairs, tables, windows, and chimneys for granted and regard electric lights, refrigerators, running water, porcelain baths, and toilets as common necessities?*

*Why did men, women, and children eke out their meager existence for 6,000 years, toiling desperately from dawn to dark - barefoot, half-naked, unwashed, unshaved, uncombed, with lousy hair, mangy skins, and rotting teeth - then suddenly, in one place on earth there is an abundance of such things as rayon underwear, nylon hose, shower baths, safety razors, ice cream sodas, lipsticks, and permanent waves?"*

Mr. Weaver then answers his question as to why we wound up with shower baths.

*"In the last analysis, all of these advantages are the natural, normal outgrowth of a political structure which unleashed the creative energies of millions of men and women by leaving them free to work out their own affairs - not under the lash of coercive authority, but through voluntary co-operation based on enlightened self-interest and moral responsibility.*

*That's why plows are now made of steel. That's why America has led the world in production accomplishments. That's why we've been able to win wars started by nations that make a regular business of fighting. That's why we are able to feed the victims of pagan aggression.*

*And last but not least, that's why the people of the United States, who occupy only 6 per cent of the world's land area and who represent less than 7 per cent of the world's population, own:*

*85 per cent of the world's automobiles*
*60 per cent of the life insurance policies*
*54 per cent of the telephones*

*48 per cent of the radio sets*
*46 per cent of the electric power capacity*
*35 per cent of the world's railway mileage*
*30 per cent of the improved highways*
*92 per cent of the modern bathtubs."*[36]

That statistic about bathtubs has changed since 1947 but we can see Weaver's point that we were the first nation to really clean up with bathtubs.

You know what? Laura and Almanzo, Caroline and Charles Ingalls, and Rose Wilder Lane all agreed with Mr. Weaver's philosophy about personal freedom and individual responsibility helping make America great.

Rose wrote this in her book *Give Me Liberty*, published in 1936, only four years after *Little House in the Big Woods* came out.

*"The telephone, the electric light, the silk stocking, fresh vegetables and fruits in winter, sanitary meat markets, the ice box, and the milk bottle, the gas range and the kerosene cookstove, ready-made clothes, the seamless sheet, wall paper, the toothbrush, the leather shoe, moving pictures, ice cream, and a thousand other things to which Americans are so accustomed that we do not see them, all testify to such a distribution of wealth in this individualistic country as no other people have dreamed of enjoying.*

*Twenty-five years ago, the automobile was a rich man's prerogative. It still is, everywhere but here. In America, the anarchy of uncontrolled individualistic selfishness has so distributed automobiles that in the worst misery of the 1930's California was overwhelmed by scores of thousands of penniless families arriving in them, and hunger marchers did not march but traveled in trucks. And these people should have automobiles; that is precisely my* point. *They should have them, and individualism has somehow, without plan or any such definite purpose, seen to it that they got them.*"[37]

Then Rose recalls the days of the Saturday night bath.

*"Thirty years ago a majority of Americans bathed in the washtub on Saturday nights and lighted their way to bed with a kerosene lamp. The English are still renowned throughout the world for their extraordinary personal cleanliness, because in every English middle-class home or upper middle-class London hotel a bath can be had in a tin tub carried to the bedroom."*[38]

When Rose wrote that, 1936, many Americans still bathed on Saturday night. Also at that time, during the Great Depression, many Americans had begun to look to government to take care of their problems, instead of having the character to face them themselves. Rose went on:

*"Today our American intellectuals point indignantly to an America which has left more than two million farm houses without modern bathrooms or electric lights. Something, they say, must be done about this. There must be more than two million American families who still use the washtub and the kerosene lamp. They should have plumbing and electricity. They should have automatic central heat, electric refrigeration, air-conditioning, television, and every other form of material wealth that may be imagined and created to serve them in the future.*

*There is still far too much economic inequality; the gap between rich and poor has not been sufficiently narrowed. Something certainly should be done to distribute wealth, to raise the general standard of living, to improve living conditions for the poor and to give everyone, particularly the rich, a more abundant life.*

*But that is precisely what this anarchy of individualism has been doing, increasingly doing for the brief time in modern history during which it has been operating. When I look as this unique American experiment which has barely begun, which has been progressing for hardly a century and a half, I think it can stand on its record."*[39]

The record is that Americans no longer take weekly Saturday night baths. The nation with the greatest individual freedoms in the history of the world has given its people the most individual benefits in the history of the world, including showers and bathtubs. But the people of this nation no longer have the spirit of the pioneers, like Ma and Pa Ingalls and Laura and Almanzo, the spirit that merged freedom with individual character and responsibility. Many people today expect their government to supply them with free cell phones, among a seemingly endless list of other things.

Laura was wise to include the details of the Saturday night baths in her books, because that custom was passing as she wrote. Her writing helped make that custom pass, because her books are chock full of freedom and individual responsibility, which showered the benefits of that freedom on America.

# Pa Ingalls, Tough as a Bear

Pa could take care of his boots himself.

Pa walked seven miles and back with a load on his back.

How far is seven miles? It may take you only about ten minutes to drive seven miles from one part of your town to another. Today that doesn't seem very far.

Pa Ingalls had to walk to town to take the furs from his winter trapping, that town was Pepin and it was seven miles away from their log home. Laura does not elaborate much on that trip, other than Pa's story of meeting what he thought was a bear on the way back home. And it does sound simple. Why elaborate? Pa merely had to walk to town and back, a nice little outing on a pleasant day.

Charles Ingalls was a pioneer. Charles Ingalls was a frontiersman. Charles Ingalls was a real man.

When Charles made his living, *he* made his living. His support of his family, Caroline, Mary, Laura and Carrie, was totally up to him. On the frontier in the Wisconsin woods, there were few jobs to be had, few companies to work for. There was no government aid or food stamp program. There were hardly even any churches, to help a family in trouble. Everything that kept them alive depended on Charles Phillip Ingalls. Each morning when he awoke, he knew that his beloved family's security and nourishment was on his shoulders. Any mistakes he made directly and immediately hurt them. Anything he got done directly helped them.

Every sunup Pa faced this decision – What will I do today to keep us all alive?

He had no co-workers. He had no union. He had no boss. He was the boss – his boss.

So what did he do?

He farmed.

Raising a successful garden takes character.

The Ingalls garden grew corn, pumpkins, turnips, squash, potatoes and carrots, among many other foods. A survival garden is different than a hobby garden, a lot bigger and a lot more important. That garden had to be plowed and planted, seeded and weeded, hoed and harvested, all in just the right way at just the right time. The weeds, bugs and worms dedicated their lives to eating the Ingalls garden before the Ingalls did. Any mistake or laziness in the gardening meant waiting a whole year – a hungry year – to do better.

Pa also raised a crop of wheat. While a garden was small, less than an acre, a wheat field was big. That field had to be plowed, with Pa wrestling the plow behind the horse. Then that broken ground had to be seeded and cultivated just right. Finally, if everything was done properly and the weather cooperated, the wheat was cut. That meant that hour after hour and day after day, Pa swung a scythe, always hurrying so the weather wouldn't ruin his crop.

In the garden and in the wheat field, sprouts and weeds always appeared, as if by magic. Those tree sprouts and wicked weeds did not have to be planted, nor did they have to be carefully tended or cultivated. They grew amazingly well all by themselves, which meant that Pa had to continually cut down weeds and dig out sprouts.

Pa also hunted. Hunting takes character. The animals that Pa hunted were accustomed to being hunted, mostly by other animals, so they took great pains not to be someone else's supper. They were skittish and wary, and just for Pa to get close to them, he had to be cleverer than they were. What's more, just to add excitement to his hunting, when Pa shot a bear, he only had one shot before the bear got him for his supper.

Pa also trapped animals for their fur. There were no polyester factories in the big woods, or Dacron or rayon. People wore furs from animals because they make the very best and warmest coats. Again, when Pa trapped those animals, they were used to being pursued and were most elusive. Pa had to work hard, trekking through deep snows, facing biting, bitter winds when he would rather have been facing a fire, as he tracked and outsmarted the animals that he trapped.

Nobody made Pa get up every morning to farm, hunt or trap. No one forced him to plow all day in the spring or cut wheat all day in the late summer. No one forced him to follow a bear's tracks when he would rather have made tracks the other way. No one forced him to slog through snow and wind in below zero weather to set his traps.

Nobody forced him to do all those things, but Pa did them.

So in *Little House in the Big Woods*, when the weather grew warmer and the temperatures crept above the melting point and the snow became soft and slushy, Pa had to carry his furs to Pepin, to get his pay for his whole winter's work.

One morning Pa headed south toward Pepin before the sun headed west in the sky. He had worked hard and the bundle of furs that he carried was almost as big as he was. Each fur by itself was not that heavy, but all the furs tightly strapped together weighed him down with their weight, so much so that he could not even carry his gun with him, as he usually did.

When he left home, the air was chilly but the snow on the ground was not frozen hard. An average person walks about three miles per hour, unburdened, meaning that it would take about two and a half hours to walk the seven miles to Pepin. But Pa was burdened, loaded down like a packhorse, trudging through the deep snow. When he stepped, he couldn't just shuffle his feet forward, with little effort. Every step had to be up and out of the snow, the slushy, heavy, compacted late winter snow that wouldn't just fluff away from his feet. Then he lunged forward and down into the snow again. Mile after mile he high-stepped his way toward town, shifting his load on his back to rest his shoulder, then shifting it back again when that one started hurting. He stopped a few times to rest his back and legs, and when he stopped, he always looked in the woods around him to see if he was being stalked by a bear or panther or wolf that wanted his fur.

It took him a long time to get to town, say four hours of lugging his load, slogging through the mushy slush. In Pepin, other trappers were ahead of him, so he had to wait his turn to trade with the storeowner. Then each fur had to be traded, one by one. What price would he give Pa, and what would Pa buy with that money?

When the sun had finished its trip through the western sky, Pa was ready to retrace his seven-mile walk. He was not burdened as before, but he had supplies to carry back to the log house, and the snow was slushier than ever, sucking on his leaden feet. The sun went to bed before Pa made it home to his. The dusky gloom meant that he could not use his eyes to watch for predators, trying to prey on him.

And somewhere in that walk, he thought he saw a bear.

*"I did not want to fight a winter-starved bear in the dark. Oh, how I wished for my gun!"*

He thought he was facing a bear without a gun, so he charged it with a tree limb instead. Then he saw that it was just a grizzled stump.

On and on he walked, listening, peering warily into the darkness, Pa Ingalls taking his little girls their candy.

He did that for the seven-mile walk back home.

But he was too late. His girls were already in bed. Giving them their candy had to wait until the next morning.

That was Pa's trip to Pepin, seven miles away from their log cabin. Was town a long ways away?

Yes, it was, a very long ways away.

But Pa Ingalls was a frontiersman, a pioneer, a man of character and will. He carried the furs for seven miles through the snow and carried their supplies seven miles back through the slush, because he had to do it. No one made him do it. No one would do it for him. But he made himself do all the things he had to do to keep his family alive, healthy and happy.

All of that was hard, wearisome work, tiring the flesh and straining the spirit. But you know what?

Pa Ingalls was alive.

He never suffered from moments of intense boredom. He never wished that the end of the day would come so that he could watch videos. He always wanted the days to be longer, so that he could get more done. Every day, he was fully wrapped up in everything he did, struggling, straining, pushing, shoving, pressing to stay alive – and being very alive while doing it.

At the end of a day, or at the end of a summer, or at the end of that seven mile walk to Pepin, Charles Phillip Ingalls had a deep satisfaction with his work, a satisfied feeling that can never come from watching someone else do something, or from doing someone else's work, or from living a life that is barely connected to reality.

Pa Ingalls was alive.

No wonder he played the fiddle so feverishly!

Pa did not need the government or anybody else looking out for him. He could take care of his own affairs, thank you.

But with the passing of the frontier, the pioneer spirit also passed.

At the end of the chapter about the two bears, Laura looked at her Pa. While he relaxed one evening, he took time to grease his boots. Years later, Laura wrote an article about how the US government, even back then, employed a high salaried bureaucrat to advise people like Pa on how to take care of their shoes.

*"The more we think for ourselves, the less we shall need advice and high priced experts would not need to waste their time and government money which is really our money, in telling us things we should think out for ourselves.*

I read an item a short time ago in a farm paper stating that government experts advised the use of oil on shoes to prolong their life and usefulness and in doing so beat the high cost of living. Full instructions were given for this treatment of shoes.

Now the weekly cleaning and greasing of the family shoes was a regular thing with the grandparents and the parents of most of us and they charged nothing for advising and instructing us in the process. In fact, there was at times a compelling quality about their advice that is lacking in that of government experts. But at least our grandparents and their "old fashioned notions" are at last vindicated.

"Scrape off all that dirt and clean those shoes up good, then rub that grease into them," said they, perhaps a bit sharply.

"The shoes should be thoroly cleaned and warm oil then rubbed well into the leather," say the experts smoothly.

So you see that expert advice was given in our homes years ago. And after all that is the best place for teaching many things, first and most important of which is how to think for one's self."[40]

What people learned on the frontier was how to think for themselves and the character to do things for themselves. One thing's for sure. Pa Ingalls did not need the government telling him how to take care of his boots. He knew how to think for himself.

*Chapter 7 (The Sugar Snow)*

# Knowing a Little about a Lot

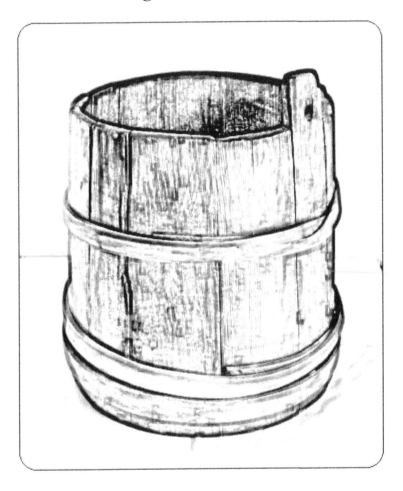

A maple sap bucket
From the family of Calvin Coolidge.
Calvin Coolidge Museum

Grandpa made his own buckets.

The "Sugar Snow" chapter is all about making maple sugar. To do that, Grandpa Ingalls, Charles' father, had to catch the sap running from the maple trees in buckets. And for that, Grandpa made his own buckets.

Did you ever know anyone who made a bucket, or could make a bucket?

Most people would kick-the-bucket before they figured out how to make one.

Grandpa, though, made his own buckets. He knew to make them out of cedar or ash wood, the woods that wouldn't give the maple sugar a bad taste. Grandpa also made little wooden troughs that went from the tree to the bucket.

Many people today might assume that people of former times did not know much and were ignominiously ignorant. Such a belief, though, would show that people of today don't know much. Pioneers lacked the machines and electronic gadgetry of today's world, but Grandpa, Caroline, and Charles Ingalls actually had a huge amount of knowledge. They had to, to do what they did.

Laura lived most of her life on a small farm, and she had absorbed much knowledge from Ma and Pa and their small farm life. She didn't realize just how much knowledge it took to live that life.

In 1919, Laura wrote an article about the life of a farmer's wife during the busy season. Consider all the knowledge that she carried into her job.

August 5, 1919, Laura Ingalls Wilder, *Missouri Ruralist*:

*"We are going to be late getting the hay in from the west meadow. Can't you come and rake it for us?" said The Man of the Place.*

*I could and did; also I drove the team on the hay fork to fill the big barn, for such is the life of a farmer's wife during the busy season."*

Notice that casual comment by Laura that she drove the team to get the hay in the barn. You do not drive a team of horses unless you know what you're doing. Dean Butler was the actor who played Almanzo in the *Little House on the Prairie* television series, and he said that, on his first day, on his first scene, when he was supposed to drive a team of horses, bad things happened.

*"[O]n my first day I nearly killed a horse when the buckboard team got away from me during my first shot."*[41]

Laura continues talking about their varied farm life skills, in the 1919 article.

*"The colt has sprained his ankle. Come pet him while I rub on some liniment, and while you are there I wish you'd look at the red heifer's bag and see what you think best to do for that swelling on it."*

*And so I halter broke the colt while The Man of the Place bathed the lame ankle and then we decided that the red heifer had been bee stung and bathed her udder with salt and water."*

Did you catch the little joke that Laura inserted there? She said she halter broke the colt while Almanzo treated its ankle. Young colts do not know that they are to stand still while someone holds them by a halter or even to stand still while tied to a post. Actually, that goes against their every instinct. Their natural response to restraint is to pull with all their might as hard as they can and run away as fast as they can. Even young horses have great strength, and if you don't know what you're doing when you handle them, you can get an unexpected visit to a doctor or dentist very quickly.

So Laura had to hold the colt while Almanzo treated its foot, and that colt did not want to be held. In fact, Almanzo wanted her to pet the colt while he worked on it, precisely because it was acting wild and wooly, so Laura said she was halter breaking it.

After Laura's little joke, she went on with her many jobs on their small farm.

*"I have finally got the weakly calf into good growing condition and turned it out in the pasture with the others, for I am by way of being an understudy for the veterinarian."*

In effect, Dr. Laura was working with all animals, great and small. Raising animals sounds simple – just put them in a pasture and watch them grow. Oh, no! It just doesn't work that way. They have to be nurtured and cared for and treated, and each different kind of animal requires a different body of knowledge about how to handle and care for that animal. A horse is different than a sheep is different than a cow is different than a goat, and working with each one takes specific knowledge of that kind and even of the individual animals, as you get to know them one by one.

Growing crops also requires great knowledge and judgment, and Almanzo sought Laura's cache of that knowledge.

*"What would you raise next year on that land we cleared of brush down by the creek? The hay on it is too thin and it must be broken*

*up." This was the question for my consideration at the breakfast table and my answer was, "Raise the same crop on that as you do on the remainder of the land on that side of the creek. One large field is better than two small ones and time is saved in working. Put it into the regular rotation with the rest."*

A government official of Laura's time, perhaps somewhat surprisingly, made a wise comment, which Laura quoted.

*"United States Commissioner of Education, Philander P. Claxton says that on a farm it is the "Know-All and Do-Everydumthing" that makes for success."*

Then Laura elaborated further on that.

*"A farmer to be successful must understand his machinery and be a sort of blacksmith. He must be a carpenter, a road builder, enough of a civil engineer to know how to handle the creeks and washouts on his farm. He must, of course, understand all about the care of the animals on the farm in sickness and in health; he must know all about the raising of crops and handling of soils, the fighting of pests and overcoming of weather conditions and in addition must be a good business man so that he shall not lose all the fruits of his toil in the buying and selling end of the game."*

In addition to all those skills, Laura, as the wife and co-operator of a small farm, also had to master all of this.

*"Besides being a helper in all these things with brains and muscle if necessary, the farmer's wife must know her own business, which includes the greatest variety of trades and occupations ever combined in one all around person. Think of them! Cook, baker, seamstress, laundrywoman, nurse, chambermaid and nurse girl. She*

*is a poultry keeper, an expert in dairy work, a specialist in canning, preserving and pickling and besides all else she must be the mother of the family and a smiling hostess."*

Laura and Almanzo actually possessed great knowledge and skills in their chosen life's work. Much of that was picked up from their parents, and Laura's books contain frequent examples of that body of wisdom.

The article "Lessons in Liberty from Laura Ingalls Wilder" comments on how Laura included so much information on how to do a lot of things.

*"In countless ways, Wilder's books aim to demonstrate by example how ordinary citizens, through the pursuit of self-reliance, can make fruitful use of the particular freedoms that existed on the frontier — and of the freedoms that all Americans have inherited as their birthright.*

*Perhaps the most consistent way in which Wilder emphasizes this theme is through the innumerable acts of self-provision described in the books. Here, today's Americans who feel that everything must be provided with some help or oversight from the state can get a confidence boost: The Little House books are replete with descriptions — some in exhaustive, "how-to" levels of detail — of the ways in which simple people with few resources manage to provide for themselves a broad array of both necessities and luxuries. Many are activities that today's adults would never dream of attempting, especially not without some kind of government regulation or aid; in Wilder's day, however, they were routinely performed by children."[42]*

Those skills were taught by parents to their children because they were skills that kept them alive, in that world at that time. That means that those children knew how to do many things that most adults today cannot do. Beyond physical skills, though, people of that time learned how to make the best out of whatever situation they faced. They often had more than pioneer skills - they had pioneer character, as the Liberty article brings out.

*"In Wilder's universe, whether one sinks or swims in the act of pioneering — or in life more generally — is thus up to each individual. "The Lord helps them that help themselves" is a constant refrain in the books; in These Happy Golden Years, when Laura is fretting about finding work as a teacher, Ma tells her: "A body makes his own luck, be it good or bad...I have no doubt you will get as good as you deserve."*

*The key to making one's own luck, of course, is in responding well to circumstances beyond one's control. Disaster may strike, and often does, but the test is in how people deal with it — in how they use their freedom to discipline themselves, drive themselves, and adapt themselves in order to provide for themselves in the face of adversity. And throughout the books, Wilder offers instruction in making lemonade out of lemons without relying on outside help."*[43]

*Little House in the Big Woods* has more information on how the Ingalls did things than any of the other books. From beginning to end, it is loaded with how-to information on basic, self-sustaining living.

In the first chapter, Laura told how Pa skinned a deer for its leather and salted and smoked the meat to preserve it. They also salted fish in barrels to preserve them and they butchered a hog. The second chapter explains how Ma churned her own butter, and the taste of homemade butter is far above today's store bought butter. Homemade is better butter!

Then in chapter three, Pa made his own bullets. In chapter four, everyone made Christmas gifts for the others, and in chapter five, Grandpa built a sled, when he was just a boy. Chapter six had Pa skinning and preserving his furs, while chapter seven showed them making maple sugar, using the buckets and troughs that Grandpa made. Chapter eight described how Grandpa had used hewn logs for the floor of his house – of course he and Charles had built their own log houses – and Aunt Ruby made a rose broach of sealing wax stuck on a broken darning needle. In chapter nine, Pa put in his crops, and each different crop required knowledge of how to plant and grow it. Somehow he also made a swing for the girls out of bark. Caroline bought fabric in Pepin to make Pa some shirts and a jumper and some white fabric to make sheets and underwear.

Chapter ten explains making cheese from the excess cow's milk, using rennet from the lining of a calf's stomach. Of course, just milking a cow can get to be an interesting experience, if you don't know what you're doing. Gathering honey from a honey bee tree without getting stung, as Pa did, also required some delicate knowledge and experience. Chapter eleven showed Pa and Uncle Henry cradling and then tying oats into sheaves, and the ladies treated Charley's bee-stung body with herbs. Chapter twelve had Ma braiding beautiful hats with oat straw, including Pa's Sunday hat, and Ma prepared delicious hulled corn, or hominy.

How much knowledge and skill and wisdom was involved in doing all those things? Chances are you don't know a single family in the whole world who can do what they did.

Perhaps we should call them Professor Caroline and Doctor Charles!

In today's world, people specialize. They learn how to do one thing very well. A person might be a computer expert, but then there are different categories of computer experts, such as software engineer or networking specialist or computer repairer. A person might be a builder, but there are many specialties in that field, such as framer, flooring installer, roofer, electrician, dry waller or plumber. One might specialize in auto mechanics, but then they often specialize further, in repairing tires, radiators, transmissions, electrical systems, or programming auto computers.

All these specialists are paid well for doing that one thing, their one skill that they learn very deeply and work at exclusively. However, then they have to get someone else to do all those other things for them – work on auto, build house, fix house, grow food, preserve food, etc.

People in Charles' and Caroline's day knew a little about a lot. People today know a lot about a little.

This is similar to the change that occurred in factories. In olden times, one man might make a product, like a piece of furniture, from beginning to end. Later, factories manufactured furniture, with each worker doing only one small part of the whole process. He didn't really build a piece of furniture. He only attached legs or painted. He was not really a furniture maker. He was only a legger or a painter. Yet this process allowed furniture to be made more quickly and at less cost.

Even automobiles were originally made as a whole project by one person, or a small group. Now they are manufactured by hundreds of corporate employees, and the job of one of those employees might just be putting a driver side door on the car.

If you took him around to the other side of the car, he would be lost. These employees are not really automobile makers. They are auto workers, little cogs in a big corporate machine that itself makes machines.

In fact, most people today are like cogs in a bigger machine, which is the worldwide economy. To be adequately paid, you must specialize in something that most people cannot do themselves. Then you must pay many other people to do things for you that you cannot do yourself. Acquiring a skill in depth gives a certain personal satisfaction. At the same time, this specialized economic system creates a massive interlocking dependence, with all the specialists depending on all the other specialists just to live.

On the other hand, Grandpa knew how to make his own buckets, Charles knew how to make bullets and deer leather, and Caroline could make head cheese and head hats. But most of all, Grandpa and Charles and Caroline knew how to stay alive without depending on anybody else to do things for them. Their farmstead was their factory and their character was their living.

When Henry Ford changed auto manufacturing from one at a time to assembly line, automobile production jumped, but worker satisfaction slumped. Just as a worker in a factory who only paints furniture does not have the same satisfaction as a craftsman who builds a whole piece of furniture, so modern specialized, dependent living does not give the same satisfaction as people whose lives were more rounded and self-sufficient. There is no way that a cedar bucket can compare to a modern automobile in value, beauty or complexity, yet in an ironic twist of time, Grandpa Ingalls probably got more satisfaction from his completed sap bucket than an auto worker does from putting a car door on a fifty thousand dollar automobile.

## Chapter 8 (Dance at Grandpa's)

# Family, Friends and Fancy Footwork

Pass through, right shoulder to right shoulder.

Grandma danced everybody down.

But everybody did dance. They all knew how, and they all loved it, the older folks, like Grandma, just as much as the younger ones, like George.

Near the end of the previous chapter, Pa announced to Caroline, with a customary twinkle in his eye, that there would be a dance. Caroline answered as she often did –

*"Oh, Charles."*

Apparently, Caroline loved dances.

Actually, everybody did.

In the big woods and throughout the frontier, life was often lonesome. Work took up almost all daylight hours, so visiting and social events were rare.

But every once in a while, there was a dance.

Towns, with churches, schools and civic organizations, naturally had more social activity. Outside the towns, though, where no two houses stood together and where neighbors were often separated not by blocks but by miles, a dance was a very special event.

Dancing's wide popularity included one famous dancer – George Washington. Unlike Grandma Ingalls in *Little House in the Big Woods*, George Washington finally reached the point where he could no longer dance. He wrote the following letter only about a month before he died at the young age of 67, declining an invitation to a dance.

*"Mount Vernon, 12th November, 1799. Gentlemen—Mrs. Washington and myself have been honored with your polite invitation to the assemblies in Alexandria this winter, and thank you for this mark of your attention. But, alas! our dancing days are no more. We wish, however, all those who have a relish for so agreeable and innocent an amusement all the pleasure the season will afford them; and I am, gentlemen,*

*Your most obedient and obliged humble servant, Geo. Washington."*

However, in his day George could have given Grandma a run for her money.

*"The same natural athletic grace he displayed while on horseback was also evident in the ballroom. Since George Washington stood much taller than most men, he was easy to spot on the dance floor as he effortlessly guided his dance partners through the intricate steps and patterns of movements required by the minuet, Virginia reel, and cotillion dances. Washington's reputation grew once again – this time as one of the best dancers in all Virginia."*[44]

George Washington's step-grandson was George Washington Parke Custis. He wrote of his grandfather's appearance at a victory ball in Fredericksburg, less than a month after the Continental victory at Yorktown in October, 1781 that ended the Revolution.

*"It was on this festive occasion that General Washington danced a minuet with Mrs. Willis... The minuet was much in vogue at that period, and was peculiarly calculated for the display of the splendid figure of the chief, and his natural grace and elegance of air and manners... As the evening advanced, the commander-in-chief yielding to the general gayety of the scene, went down some dozen couple in the contre dance with great spirit and satisfaction."*[45]

So everyone from the first president of the country down to little Laura Ingalls enjoyed country dances. "Dance at Grandpa's" is perhaps the liveliest chapter in Laura's big woods book. The ride to Grandpa's house is given in vivid detail, with the early morning yellow light streaking through the tree trunk shadows and making a pinkish hue on the fresh and frozen snow. They passed cottontail rabbit tracks spread far apart in hops, little bitty snowbird tracks that Laura described as featherstitching, and fox and deer tracks. Grandpa's house and making the maple syrup are also described in elaborate detail.

And then came the music and the dancing!

From Laura's lively descriptions, everybody had a fantastic time at those dances! No wonder that, when Pa announced the dance to Caroline, she answered as she did.

Then Caroline had an announcement of her own to make – *she would wear her delaine dress.*

That said it all. For this dance at Grandpa's house, Caroline would wear her most elegant attire, made by a professional dressmaker back on the east coast, a dress that Laura and Mary had never even seen their mother wear and had only touched one time –

Her beautiful delaine dress.

*Encyclopedia Britannica says "delaine, (French: "of wool") any high-grade woolen or worsted fabric made of fine combing wool. Delaine was originally a high-quality women's wear dress material. The word delaine is still applied to a staple all-wool fabric made in plain weave and of compact structure. Delaine sheep, a Merino type, are raised in the United States, Australia, New Zealand, Germany, Poland, and to a lesser extent in France."[46]*

*The Old Farmer's Almanac* comments on Caroline's fancy dress this way.

*"It's a kind of woolen fabric that Caroline Ingalls' East Coast dressmakers used to make her fancy dress before she traveled out West with Charles, in "Little House on the Prairie." She'd probably kept it packed away in moth repellent herbs (bay, cedar, pennyroyal, sage or even tobacco) in between barn dances. It was likely well-tailored and fitted at the bodice, then cut wide in the skirts. The word*

*comes from the French "de" for of, and "laine" for wool. There's a breed of sheep of pure Merino descent, with a very smooth body and long fine fleece that was particularly used for these finer woolen fabrics. Sometimes the wool was woven together with cotton before making it into a dress fabric, but more often the delaine was 100 percent wool. It might have been dyed in the wool, before weaving, or fabric-dyed with a plain or even fancy flowered print, or possibly embroidered after the dressmaking was completed. It must have been hot for dancing in, though, especially with all the petticoats underneath!"[47]*

We can only observe that if Laura had never seen Ma in that dress, that meant they hadn't had dances at Grandpa's before. We also note that Caroline could still fit into the dress that she wore before she was married, even after having three babies. Being overweight was not a problem on the frontier.

What a dress that must have been for Laura to have remembered it as she did, with the little strawberry pattern and dark red buttons, and whalebone in the seams.

Whale bones?

The University of Aberdeen, Scotland comments stiffly on the use of whalebone in women's fashion.

*"By far the most important use of whale-bone from the Greenland fishery was as a stiffening element in various items of fashionable attire. Whales and women were intimately associated for over 300 years, to the severe detriment of both. Whales died painful deaths that women might live painful, but fashionable lives.*

*Throughout the middle ages women enjoyed loose fitting, free flowing dresses. This all changed around the beginning of the 16th century when the unadorned lines of mediaeval clothing evolved into moulded shapes. The focus of attention for the next 300 years was to be the waist with women aiming for the smallest possible. In this they were helped by a variety of devices, such as corsets, all stiffened with bands of ivory, wood and even iron, but most successfully by slats of whale-bone. At the same time, the lower part of the body was covered in voluminous skirts and petticoats which by contrast made the waist appear even smaller. At various times in history these were so large that they required support on various frames or cages known as farthingales or crinolines. Again, whale-bone was the ideal material for their production, being light, strong and flexible."*[48]

Charles' sisters Docia and Ruby struggled into their corsets under their dresses, but Caroline may have had a corset sewn right into her dress, with the whale bones.

Caroline also wore a gold collar pin, a fit accessory for such a fine dress.

Dancing takes a lot of room, so it's good that Grandpa had a big house, at least bigger than the Ingalls' cabin. Even so, it's likely that the dancers had to take turns getting on the floor to take their turns around the floor.

Unfortunately, Pa never made it on the floor. He was the fiddler.

What's the difference between a fiddler and a violinist?

The same difference as between supper and dinner.

When the Normans from France conquered England in 1066 AD, the French speaking Normans were the upper class and the Old English speaking Anglos were the lower class. The

Normans ate dinner as their evening meal and heard music from a violin. The Anglos ate supper as their evening meal and listened to fiddle music.

Pa Ingalls played a fine fiddle, but that meant he didn't get to dance!

The fiddle is a small instrument but its music will carry across the top of a crowd of dancers. The bow rubbing hard on the strings creates a searing screech that in the hands of a skilled player comes out as wonderful music. No other stringed instrument, whether guitar, banjo or mandolin, can carry and hold the melody like a fiddle –

Unless it's a violin.

The fiddle has a small fingerboard, allowing rapid noting. Thus the fiddle is well suited for playing fast, rhythmic dance tunes. A dictionary says that "fiddle" can be a verb that means, *"To move one's fingers or hands in a nervous fashion,"* because that's exactly what fiddlers do when they play.[49]

And the sound of a fiddle, playing one of those get-up-and-get-along jigs, just absolutely forces your feet to do things they wouldn't ordinarily do. When a fiddler starts playing a jig or a reel, your legs lose their tiredness, your mind loses its melancholy and your feet lose their gravity. Every time!

Fiddlers love to fiddle, even if they don't get to dance. That's how they learned to fiddle to begin with, because they loved it so much they just couldn't stop, and kept playing until they learned it. Dance jigs have so many little fiddle notes that they are difficult to learn because those hundreds of notes are jammed together so closely. To learn each song, it must be listened to carefully, taking one small section at a time. Pa Ingalls had done that, learning from old timers who had learned from old timers before them.

And you'd better believe that at a dance, Pa Ingalls was a very popular fellow. They couldn't even have a dance without him.

If Charles didn't dance, what did poor Caroline do?

She danced! Apparently, Martha Washington did not dance, for whatever reason, so George danced with many other ladies. A dance was not a romantic event and there was no close embracing as in later dances. That kind of country dancing was cerebral, exercising the mind just as much as the body. So Caroline would have danced with other partners, while Charles was fiddling.

Many American dances were brought over from England, Ireland and Scotland.

*"Country dances are performed in three characteristic formations: (1) circular, for an indefinite number of couples ("round" dances), (2) "longways" set, double-file line for an indefinite number of couples, men on one side, women on the other, and (3) geometric formations (e.g., squares, triangles) or sets, usually for two, three, or four couples. The dancers execute a succession of varied patterns of figures. In "progressive-longways" dances, continuous interchange brings a new leading couple to the head of the set with each repetition of the pattern of figures. Round and longways dances predominate in the folk tradition. Longways and geometric sets are more frequent among courtly dances.*

*"English colonists carried them to North America, where they began a new folk-dance tradition as the "contra," or longways dance (e.g., the Virginia reel), and, in modified form, as the American square dance."[50]*

It is often said that George Washington's favorite dance was the Sir Roger de Coverley, from which came the Virginia Reel, as dances tend to change with time and geography.

*"Evidently, he (George Washington) was quite the dandy. He loved dancing to distraction. He enjoyed the minuet, popular among the social elite, but would anyone care to guess what his favorite dance was? George Washington favored Sir Roger de Coverley, which we today know as the Virginia Reel."[51]*

A gentleman seldom danced with only one lady all night long. Instead, each lady planned her dances with different partners for the different dances throughout the evening, and she seldom refused a gentleman's request to be her partner. Sometimes, if not enough gentlemen were present or involved, ladies would dance with other ladies as their partners. In fact, this type of dance often has each lady dancing with every gentleman on the floor, and each gent dances with each lady.

Talk about a social occasion!

So for the Virginia Reel, which they most likely included at the dance at Grandpa's, Ma probably was asked to dance by Uncle George. Pa said that Uncle George was wild after he returned from the Civil War, although he had been back for several years, so this reel was a fitting dance for wild George.

What would that dance have been like?

Let's imagine.

George began the dance by courteously escorting Caroline to the center of the room, where the ladies and gentlemen dancers formed two lines facing each other. As the music began, the gentlemen bowed to the ladies and the ladies curtseyed in return. We will assume that since Pa was playing the music, someone else would have called this dance, although apparently Pa did some playing and calling at the same time, which requires two hands and two brains.

Caroline and George were the top couple, at the head of the line of several couples. When the caller said, "right hand swing," George took Caroline's right hand in his and they swung to the other side of the line and then back. A left hand swing mirrored that. Do-si-do had the dancers folding their arms in front of them and passing their partners back to back. A two-hand swing was a little more vigorous, as wild George swung Caroline with both hands, and if her hair had been down instead of put up, it would have stood out behind her. After the wild two-hand swing, even though she was a somewhat demure woman, Caroline couldn't help streaming a big smile across her face.

"Top couple down and back," shouted the caller over the frenetic fiddling.

George took Caroline's hands in his and they skipped from their end of the line to the other end, and then back to the top of the line. There they joined right arms at the elbows and George swung half way round, then George turned to the next lady in line, joined left arms with her and swung her one turn around. Caroline did the same with the next gentleman in the men's line, then swung back to the center where wild George and she swung with right arms together, then back to the next person in each line for left arms, then again back to the partner. That continued all the way down the line, except –

Always, with all the whirling and spinning around from dancer to dancer and from the partner to the line to the partner to the line – someone gets confused! So halfway through the line, wild George turned Caroline one-half turn too far, then turned around to the wrong line, and wound up trying to swing Grandpa.

Grandpa was not amused!

Well, actually he was amused, as was everyone else in the line and in the room. When George or whoever turns to the wrong line and tries to dance with Grandpa instead of a lady, that is funny.

Caroline and George breathed rapidly, their cheeks glowed red, and their smiles spread all across their faces as they swung around and around with each other and all the others on their line as they reeled the set. Their feet stayed on beat, the fiddle music sang sweet, and as long as the reel music kept going there was no way they could slow their feet down. Wild George bounced so high off the floor with each step that even the log slabs under his frantic feet moved in rhythm. While the top couple was whirling and reeling through the lines, the other couples in those lines clapped in rhythm when they weren't whirling, waiting for their turn to be top couple.

When Caroline and George had reeled through every dancer in line, at the bottom of the lines they joined hands and skipped through the center back to the top again. At the top, they curled around the outside of the line and headed back to the bottom, with everyone else curling out and following them, the ladies following Caroline and the gentlemen following George. At the bottom of the line, Caroline and George formed an arch, and all the other partners joined hands and skipped through the arch, then reformed the two lines. That left Caroline and George at the bottom of the line, and it was someone else's turn to be top couple and reel the set.

When all couples had reeled the set, the dance was over. They applauded the fiddler and they laughed deeply, as the dancing in their feet freed the joy in their spirits. Then all the gentlemen, including wild George, courteously escorted the ladies back to their seats on the side of the room, thanked them for the dance, and walked away to find another partner.

Laura mentioned that at some point during the dance, Uncle George did a pigeon wing, a fancy step where he threw out one leg, as a pigeon stretches out his wing, then slapped his feet together and stood facing his mother. She answered his choreographic challenge and then they jigged, as their feet clogged on the wood floor, their upper bodies hardly moving, their feet and legs moving but hardly visible with their rapid motion. And Grandma danced George down! George being a healthy young man, that meant that Grandma danced everybody else down, too.

Laura loved the dance at Grandpa's house, probably one of several that they enjoyed. The woods had been covered with snow for so long! A dance like that just before springtime broke down the walls of winter and was obviously a night to remember. Laura did remember that night, and even though she was a little girl, she carried minute details with her all those years, of the music, the dances, and the fun, as she later wrote –

*"The dancing was so pretty and the music so gay that Laura knew she could never get tired of it. All the beautiful skirts went swirling by, and the boots went stamping, and the fiddle kept on singing gaily."*[52]

# Going to Town to Go to Town

Going to town, riding slowly behind the horses.

When the Ingalls went to town, Laura got excited.

Actually, everybody got excited. Going to town was a big event.

It was such a big event that we have an idiom left over from that time.

Today most people live in a town or a city. Those who don't, live close to a town or city, so most people are in a town almost every day. Actually, today it's a bigger event to get out of town than it is to go to town. 'Hey, we're going to the country!'

But before the twentieth century, going to town was such a big event that the English language has the idiom –

to 'go to town;'

or 'going to town.'

The dictionary says that to 'go to town' is *"to do something eagerly and as completely as possible; or to make a supreme or unrestricted effort; go all out. Angie and Phil have really gone to town on their wedding."*[53]

Why do we have that saying? Because when families went to town, they really put themselves into it. They went all out to go to town. So when we say that the Ingalls were "Going to Town to Go to Town," we mean they put forth a lot of effort to get ready to go to town.

Why was going to town such a big event?

Apart from the big cities, very few people lived in towns. People didn't travel much, to go to town or anywhere else. A team of horses pulling a wagon might walk at a pace of four miles per hour, about fifteen minutes per mile, so it took a long time to travel anywhere. A horse pulling a buggy might go a little faster, but then most of the people who owned buggies lived in town, anyway.

In Laura's Ozarks, where she lived from 1894 until 1957, the little towns are situated by drive time – horse and wagon drive time. From Mansfield, Ava is fourteen miles south, Seymour is twelve miles west, Hartville is twelve miles north, and Norwood is ten miles east. The towns are positioned like that because a family could drive five to seven miles into town, do their trading, and then drive back home for evening chores.

People didn't see other people very much. They had a lot of work and little social activity. Rose Wilder Lane explains what life was like at the end of the 1800's, including what a big deal it was to go to town.

*"There were no cars, no highways, no radios or planes, no movies, no tall buildings, no electric lights, no toothpaste, not many toothbrushes, no soda fountains, no bottled soft drinks, no hot-dog stands, no High Schools, no low shoes, no safety razors or shaving cream, no green vegetables in the wintertime and none in cans, no bakers' bread or cakes or doughnuts, no dime stores, no super-markets. An orange was a Christmas treat, in prosperous families. There was no central heating, and only the very prosperous had bathtubs; they were tin or zinc, encased in mahogany in the homes of the very rich. The rich, too, had gas-lights. Some streets in the largest cities were lighted, with gas-lamps. Spring came to American children when mama let them go barefoot. No moderately prosperous parents thought of letting children wear out good shoe-leather in the summertime. Stockings were cotton. Sheets were made at home, of muslin seamed down the center, for looms had never made muslin as wide as a bed. Mother made all the family's clothes, except Father's best suit, and sometimes she still made that. Forty years ago, a journey of ten miles to the next town (by buggy or mail-hack or*

train) was planned and prepared for, at least some weeks in advance."[54]

In her book *Old Home Town*, Rose remembered the time when she was a little girl, one generation later than Laura. By then, people went to town once a week, instead of once a year as Laura wrote about in *Little House in the Big Woods*.

*"Country folks wore their best clothes when they came to town. The journey of two or eight miles was not to be undertaken on the spur of the moment. During the week the horses were working in the fields or the men were too busy to hitch up. A farm woman could harness the old mare and sometimes did, but dealing with horses was felt to be a man's work...*

*On Saturdays they came to town, dressed for the occasion and bringing the week's surplus of butter, eggs, vegetables and fruits. They came to the stores, to trade.*

*The word lingers, though its meaning has been forgotten. Americans who never bartered eggs for calico will say, "I trade at So-and-So's," or, "He gets my trade." In those days, the small towns had never heard of going shopping.*

*From east and west the main-traveled roads came into town."*

Rose said that "*Spring came to American children when mama let them go barefoot.*" Why did children like to go barefoot? Sometimes bare, grassless ground was too hot to be comfortable on bare feet, and sometimes pebbles or gravels were too sharp to be walked on, and going without shoes always meant a toe badly stubbed on a rock or root. On the other hand, feeling bare toes squished down into lush green grass and feet flying over the turf was truly one of the memorable little pleasures in life.

Children's shoes had to last a whole year. If they were bought in the fall, by the next summer they would inevitably be one size too small and worn thin on the bottom. So when spring came in the big woods, it was time for Mary and Laura to go barefoot, and it was time for the whole family to go to town. Going to town even meant bathing in the middle of the week. It is unclear if they bathed again on Saturday, or if they stretched that mid-week bath out until the next Saturday.

Mary's and Laura's hair was twisted up in little bits of rag, to give it curl, so the girls could look their very prettiest for the townsfolk. They wore their best dresses, a blue calico for Mary and a dark red calico for Laura. Ma did not wear her very best delaine dance dress, of course, but she did wear what must have been her second best, a brown calico, and she wore the same gold collar pin that she had worn to the dance. Pa wore his 'good' shirt, instead of one of the others, which were not so good.

Since the snow had melted and the roads had shed their load of snowdrifts and icy ruts, the family took the wagon into town, swept clean as one might vacuum a car. Pa also took extra time to curry the horses. Back and forth he went with the currycomb on their fine horse hair, and their shaggy winter hair came off in clumps. The teeth of the comb brought up oil from the horses' skin, until their coat was handsome enough for a town trip. That was kind of like washing and waxing the car today before a big trip.

To travel seven miles to town on a wagon pulled by a team of horses took about two hours. When Laura lived at Mansfield, Missouri, sometimes she and Almanzo drove a team of horses up to Hartville, twelve miles away, so Laura could participate in a women's club. That trip took three hours each way. So to go seven miles to Pepin would take them almost two hours, like driving over a hundred miles today.

Near the end of their two-hour wagon ride, Laura began to catch glimpses of blue water through the trees. Then the trees stopped and the river valley began, and Laura saw Lake Pepin by the village of Pepin.

The lake and the town took the name of two early French explorers, brothers Pierre and Jean Pepin, who came down from Canada about 1679. Pepin was an old village, but the village was not platted or laid out until 1855, just twelve years before Laura was born. Pepin was one of only two villages in Pepin County. Durand lay to the east of the Ingalls cabin, about twice as far away as Pepin, and at that time, Durand had about seven hundred residents. Pepin had about five hundred, a good-sized village, perhaps even big enough to be called a town, as Laura did.

There were six post offices in the county, twenty-six schools, one of which Laura and Mary actually attended for a short while, although not mentioned in the big woods book, and only four churches, making it difficult for most people to attend church.

Unlike most lakes, the lake that Laura saw was made by God, not people. Just below Pepin, the Chippewa River flows into the Mississippi. That delta area of the Chippewa narrows the Mississippi channel down to only about a quarter of a mile wide. Above that area, the river naturally backs up and spreads out, creating Lake Pepin.

Reads Landing, Minnesota, is south of Pepin by the narrow part of the river. A plaque there tells how the lake came to be.

*"Lake Pepin occupies the Mississippi Valley above this point for a distance of 22 miles. The lake is formed by the delta of the Chippewa River which enters the Mississippi directly east of this site.*

*The Chippewa, a relatively small river, has a much steeper gradient than that of the Mississippi. It was therefore able to transport more sand and coarser gravel than the master stream could remove. In consequence the Mississippi was dammed back in the gorge to form Lake Pepin.*

*The surface of the lake is 664 feet above sea level and 450 feet below the top of the bluffs which line its shores…*

*The bottom of the gorge is 150 feet below the lake surface having been filled to its present elevation as the carrying power of the river decreased."*[55]

That was the Mississippi River that Laura saw, flowing lazily along while hardly seeming to flow at all, lying wide and calm like a lake for a length of twenty-two to twenty-eight miles, depending on who's measuring, and up to three miles wide from the Wisconsin side of the river to the other side in Minnesota.

The Mississippi River flows from northern Minnesota by the states of Wisconsin, Iowa, Illinois, Missouri, Kentucky, Tennessee, Arkansas, Mississippi and Louisiana, all the way to the Gulf of Mexico, a course of over 2300 miles. Yet when Laura looked at the Lake Pepin part of the Mississippi, she was looking at the widest part of the whole river.

And she was also looking at the most beautiful, as Explore Wisconsin explains.

*"The steep hills and deep valleys have a quiet, wild beauty that has inspired artists and writers for more than a century, including Mark Twain and William Cullen Bryant, a late 19th century visitor, who wrote, Lake Pepin ... "ought to be visited in the summer by every poet and painter in the land." The Rochester Post-Bulletin praised the county's charm, editorializing that "Pepin and Stockholm, tucked between the bluffs and river are blessed with one of the more scenic settings in the Midwest. And ... they are relatively untouched by the kind of crass commercial development that turns charm into a curse." The New York Times travel editor wrote of Pepin County, "This back county has an untouched quality, as if [it] is dreaming of early pioneer days, when the wilderness came down to the edge of the fields." "*[56]

A few years before Laura wrote about Lake Pepin in her big woods book, the lake was already a place of note. Lake City is another town on Lake Pepin, north of Pepin and over on the Minnesota side of the river. This plaque stands in Lake City.

*"I decided that if you could ski on snow, you could ski on water." In 1922, after first trying barrel staves, then snow skis, eighteen year old Ralph W. Samuelson succeeded in waterskiing on eight foot long pine boards, steamed in boiling water to curve the tips. During the next fifteen years, Samuelson put on one-man waterskiing exhibitions, donating most of the admission charges to Lake City for the purchase of harbor and park land. Because of Samuelson's pioneering efforts in this popular sport, the American Water Ski Association in 1966 officially recognized Lake City as the birthplace of waterskiing."*

Although the water skiing fame came first, Lake Pepin is far better known because of Laura's books. Mr. Samuelson, who was not on the lake when Laura visited and did not make it into her books, did make it into the Water Ski Hall of Fame. On July 8, 1925, he became the first water ski jumper, again accomplishing his feat on Lake Pepin.[57]

Laura remembered a big log building on the edge of the lake where Pa traded. Behind that store, Laura saw many other houses. Farther down the lake, but not mentioned in her book, a huge house rose up on Harbor Hill. That house was built in 1870, not long before Laura's visit, a handsome Queen Anne style Victorian home, built for the daughter of an attorney from another town in Wisconsin. One wing of the house faces the lake, approached by wide steps that walk up the hill, and that part of the house has a downstairs porch and an upstairs porch. Behind that, another wing of the house runs at a right angle to the first, and joining the two is a round tower that rises high in the sky, with windows all the way around. That was a new house when the Ingalls visited town, it was the showplace of Pepin, the Ingalls probably drove by it, and couldn't help but notice that it was quite different from the little log house that they lived in.

The Ingalls had a picnic by the beautiful lake and spent a wonderful afternoon there, in that lovely spot, so close to and so far away from the dark, big woods. Near the end of the day, they began their two-hour wagon ride back home. As they looked back behind them, and surely they did, the sun set far beyond the other side of Lake Pepin, somewhere over on the edge of Minnesota. Soon they were again surrounded by trees and deer and rabbits and bears and panthers, but Pa had his gun and he knew how to use it, so they all felt safe as dusk settled into the thick forest and they all waddled home in their wagon.

As noted before, their two-hour wagon ride to go seven miles is like a hundred mile car ride today in the time it takes, but the rides are similar in no other ways.

The evening air became cool, so Ma, Pa, Mary, and Laura pulled their wraps around them, because they were all outside in that evening air. The rising moon filtered down through the trees, giving more shadows than light, but covering everything with a magical moonglow. The wagon wheels turned almost silently on the worn dirt road, and the horses' feet beat out a steady, soft rhythm, not fast, just plodding. Pa sat with the driving lines in his hands, but the horses knew where they were going as well as he did and wanted to get back home just as much as he did, so the lines were limp. Ma sat beside Pa, holding baby Carrie warm and secure in her arms. Mary and Laura sat behind them, under all the moon and stars and tree shadows, just sitting there for two whole hours, with nothing but God and his creation and each other to keep them company.

No car trip today is ever like that.

They talked. They thought. They sat. They absorbed the creation that was around them, that they were a part of, that became a part of them.

Soon the little log cabin welcomed them home again. The big day was over. It would be a long time before they would go to town again.

Many years later, after she had become a famous author of renowned children's books, a friend of Laura's recalled when she went into town, the town of Mansfield, Missouri, not much larger than Pepin.

*"Editor: Mrs. Dennis, you used to see Laura and Almanzo in the forties when they came into the grocery store where you worked.*

*Peggy: Yes. I worked in the H. C. Pennington Grocery Store. Then later it became the MFA Store and Mr. Pennington managed it for them.*

*Editor: What can you recall about seeing Laura in those days?*

*Peggy: When Laura came into the grocery store where I worked, she was always dressed up. She dressed simply but she was attractive. Laura wore black a lot, and she would wear long, jet black bead necklaces and little, long black earrings that dangled. She always wore a hat, even though it wasn't in style then. For a while there, you know, a lot of women wore hats. She always came in every Wednesday to do her shopping.*

*In the grocery store back then, you handed your list to the clerk and they got your order while you waited. So when Laura came into the store every Wednesday, we got her a little box to sit on while we got her groceries.*

*Editor: I can visualize this lovely, little old lady – raised by Ma Ingalls to be prim, proper and dignified – wearing formal black with a small black hat cocked on her smooth white hair, sitting on a wooden box while she waits for her groceries. One of the most famous writers in the country sitting on a wooden box waiting for her groceries, every Wednesday in Mansfield, Missouri."*

Even then, going to town was a big event for Laura.

*Chapter 10 (Summertime)*

# So Glad You Came

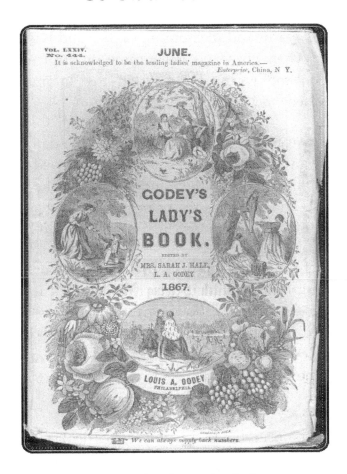

A copy of *Godey's Lady's Book*,
Such as Caroline and Mrs. Huleatt
looked at together on their visits.

In olden times, when people dropped by for a visit, they did not text or message or even call ahead of time. They just showed up.

"Hi, there!"

Summertime was the time to work in the fields, so Pa got too tired to even play his fiddle. It was the time to make cheese, because the cows gave so much milk – the Ingalls were in Wisconsin, you know. And summertime was the time to visit. The air was warm and pleasant, not bitter and blustery as in the winter when Eliza and Peter came over for a visit and shivered on the wagon ride. So in the summer, people traveled to see their neighbors, just to visit.

After one visit from Aunt Lotty, who was the daughter born to Caroline's widowed mother after she re-married, Laura got in big trouble. Lotty told Mary and Laura that she liked both golden curls and brown curls. Later, when Mary asserted the superiority of her own golden curls, Laura slapped her.

That incident made a strong impression on Laura, and she wrote a long article about it, which is included in our book *Laura Ingalls Wilder's Most Inspiring Writings*. That article had a somewhat different tone than the incident in the big woods book. It's doubtful that Aunt Lotty ever knew what a lot of trouble came after her visit, when she was just trying to be nice.

Visiting in pioneer times was a joy, particularly when the visitor was extended family, a brother or sister or parent or cousin. Pioneers didn't have visitors often, because they really didn't have much time to visit. They all had their work to do, which they never quite caught up on. Sometimes, though, the urge to visit just couldn't be resisted, and the need to see someone special couldn't be overcome without actually seeing him or her. That's when Uncle Henry or Uncle George or Grandpa or some other dear person came by Caroline and Charles' place – just for a visit.

That visit would be on a day when Ma and Pa were busy at their normal work, because Ma and Pa were always busy at their normal work. Suddenly, in the middle of the day, out of the woods and right in front of the house, Uncle Henry or Uncle George or Grandpa or neighbor Mrs. Huleatt popped up.

"Hi, Grandpa!" one of the girls might yell.

And the Ingalls had a visitor!

Even though it might not be very convenient, and even though Ma might have wanted to get that batch of cheese finished or Pa might have wanted to get the rest of that field cultivated, they immediately dropped everything and changed their schedule. They had a visitor! Their guest came first. The welcome mat was out, so the work stopped and the visiting started.

The family invited the visitor to eat with them. To neglect to invite a guest to dinner or supper would have been the crudest of manners. On the other hand, a guest could hardly refuse to stay for the meal, even if he really did have somewhere else he had to go. That would almost have been an insult.

During most visits, then, the guest shared a meal with his hosts. For that meal, the Ingalls set their company table, with store-bought sugar. When company came, the family put away their maple sugar, delicious as it was, and brought out their small supply of purchased sugar. In turn, when Caroline and Charles visited Uncle Henry or Grandpa or the Huleatts, the hosts put away their maple sugar and set the fancy sugar on the table. Serving store-bought sugar was a way of showing guests how special they were. This shows that people couldn't visit too often, because they couldn't afford all that expensive sugar.

Laura said in chapter nine that their store-bought sugar was light brown, not white as most sugar is today. The brown sugar was raw, unrefined sugar and because of its higher molasses content, actually had more nutrients in it than common white sugar.

To accommodate the drop-in visitor, Ma had to scurry and put extra food in the pot. She did not normally cook enough to have leftovers, because they had no way of keeping them and they certainly did not want to waste food. So to feed the extra mouths, Ma had to cook extra food, making sure there were extra portions for everyone.

To have a mealtime guest was a special treat for a family. During the special meal, they all sat and ate and visited. The TV was not blaring in the den. No radio was playing in the kitchen. There was nothing going on, the house was totally quiet, and all attention was focused on the visitor. The family talked with their guest; they actually visited with the visitor; they had an extended, pleasant, relaxed conversation.

After all, that's what visiting is.

Sometimes Laura and Mary visited their closest neighbors, the Petersons, who lived across the road and down the hill. They were close enough that the two little girls could walk there by themselves and visit with Mrs. Peterson. Those visits were unusual because Mrs. Peterson spoke no English and the girls spoke no Swedish, as Mrs. Peterson did. Obviously, the Petersons had recently moved to America from Sweden, as did a number of immigrants about that time. Some 60,000 Swedes left their homeland during the three years of 1867-69 as a result of severe famines with many settling in Wisconsin. In 1895, the small community of Lund was big enough to be listed in an *Atlas of Pierce County, Wisconsin*.[58] Swedish immigrants settled Lund, named it after the city of Lund, Sweden, and it is only about a mile from the Ingalls' cabin. In 1872, the Swedish Methodist Church was built and still stands at Lund.

*"This Swedish Methodist Church was built in 1872 by Swedish pioneers on an acre of land deeded by Anders and Carolina Johnson, Swedish immigrants from the province of Varmland, Sweden. The Methodist Church was on the Lund Circuit of the Northern Swedish Mission Conference of Methodist Churches, and served as the central church in the area. Swedish speaking pastors served the parishioners, traveling by horse and buggy. Some of the original members who worshiped here are buried in the cemetery behind the church."*[59]

Swedish immigrants also organized the Lund Mission Covenant Church in 1874.[60] So Laura's Swedish neighbor probably attended one of those churches.

Sometimes a neighbor or a relative sent a message that a visit was planned on a certain day – for all day. That gave Caroline time to clean and cook and prepare. When the day of the visit came, all could sit back and relax and –

Visit.

Again, there were no gadgets of any kind to distract from the pleasant conversation. The whole day was taken up with conversation.

Surely people of former, pre-electronic times developed the art of conversation far above what is common today.

In Tolstoy's *War and Peace*, the hostess was responsible for feeding the conversation, as one might feed a fire to keep it going. *"And having got rid of this young man who did not know how to behave, she resumed her duties as hostess and continued to listen and watch, ready to help at any point where the conversation might happen to flag."*

And in Jane Austen's *Pride and Prejudice*, some of Jane and Elizabeth Bennet's 'friends' were adept at conversing. *"When the ladies removed after dinner, Elizabeth ran up to her sister, and seeing her well guarded from cold, attended her into the drawing-room, where she was welcomed by her two friends with many professions of pleasure; and Elizabeth had never seen them so agreeable as they were during the hour which passed before the gentlemen appeared. Their powers of conversation were considerable. They could describe an entertainment with accuracy, relate an anecdote with humour, and laugh at their acquaintance with spirit."*

Many years after the cabin in the big woods, but still before Laura had written her books, she gave an example of a conversation between her and her friends, who were visiting at Rocky Ridge.

*"A group of friends was gathered around a glowing fire the other evening. The cold outside and the warmth and cheer and soft lights within had opened their hearts and they were talking freely together as good friends should.*

"I propose that we eliminate the word can't from our vocabularies for the coming year," said Mrs. Betty. "There ain't no such animile anyhow."

"But sometimes we just c—" began Sister Sue, then stopped abruptly at the sound of an amused chuckle.

"Oh, well—if you feel that way about it!" rejoined Mrs. Betty, "but I still insist that if you see such an animal it is only a creature of the imagination. When I went to school they tried to teach me that it was noble to say, 'I'll try' when confronted with a difficult thing to be done, but it always sounded weak to me. Why! the very expression presupposes failure," she went on with growing earnestness. "Why not say I will, and then make good? One can, you know, for if there is not one way to do a thing there are usually two."

"That word 'can't' with its suggestion of failure!" exclaimed George. "Do you know a man came up to me on the street the other day and said, "You can't lend me a dollar, can you?" He expected to fail in his request—and he most certainly did," he added grimly.

"After all," said brother James slowly, "people do a good deal as they are expected to do, even to saying the things they are expected to say. the power of suggestion is very strong. Did you ever notice how everyone will agree with you on the weather? I have tried it out many a time just for fun. Before the days of motor cars, when we could speak as we passed driving along the road, I have said to the first man I met, 'This is a fine day,' and regardless of what the weather might be, he never would fail to answer, 'Sure, it's a fine day,' or something to that effect and pass on smiling. To the next man I met I would say, 'Cold weather we're having,' and his reply would always be, 'Coldest I ever knew at this season,' or 'Mighty cold this morning,' and he would go on his way shivering. No matter if it's raining a man usually will agree with you that it's awfully dry weather, if you suggest it to him right."

"Speaking of friends," said Philip, which no one had been doing tho all could trace the connecting thought, "Speaking of friends—I heard a man say not long ago that he could count all the friends he had on the fingers of one hand. I wonder"—and his voice trailed off into silence as his thought carried him away. A chorus of protest arose.

"Oh, how awful!" exclaimed Pansy, with the tender eyes. "Anyone has more friends than that. Why, if everybody is sick or in trouble everybody is his friend."

"It all depends on one's definition of friend," said Mrs. Betty in a considering tone. "What do we mean when we say 'friend'? What is the test for a friend?" A silence fell upon the little group around the glowing fire.

"But I want to know," insisted Mrs. Betty. "What is the test for a friend? Just what do you mean Philip, when you say, 'He is my friend'?"

"Well, "Philip replied, "when a man is my friend I expect he will stand by me in trouble, that he will do whatever he can do to help me if I am needing help and do it at once even at cost of inconvenience to himself."

"Now, Pansy! How do you know your friends?" still insisted Mrs. Betty.

"My friends," said Pansy, with the tender eyes, "will like me anyway, no matter what my faults are. They will let me do as I please and not try to change me but will be my friends whatever I do."

"Next," began Mrs. Betty, but there were exclamation from every side. "No! No! It's your turn now! We want to know what your test of friendship is!"

"Why! I was just asking for information," answered Mrs. Betty with a brilliant smile, the warmth of which included the whole circle. "I wanted to know—"

"Tell us! Tell us!" they all insisted.

"Well, then," earnestly, "my friends will stand by me in trouble. They will love me even tho I make mistakes and in spite of my faults, but if they see me in danger of taking the wrong course they will warn me. If necessary, they will even tell me of a fault which perhaps is growing on me unaware. One should dare anything for a friend, you know."

"Yes, but to tell friends of a fault is dangerous," said gentle Rosemary. "It is so likely to make them angry."

"To be sure," Mrs. Betty answered. "But if we are a friend we will take it thankfully for the sake of the spirit in which it is given as we do a Christmas present which otherwise we would not care for."

> "Remember well and bear in mind
> A constant friend is hard to find
> And when you find one good and true
> Change not the old one for the new."

quoted Philip as the group began to break up.

"No, don't change 'em," said George, in the bustle of the putting on of wraps. "Don't change 'em! Just take 'em all in!"[61]

That's visiting – having a pleasant, compelling conversation with one's guests, with the warmth in the room coming from more than the fire.

Laura mentioned that a neighbor, Mrs. Huleatt, came to visit. The Huleatts were good friends with Caroline and Charles and came over often. Their children Eva and Clarence played well with Mary and Laura, and Ma even made a comment once relating to Laura and Clarence someday possibly getting married.[62] During their visit, Caroline and her guest Mrs. Huleatt would sit quietly, looking at *Godey's Lady's Book* that Mrs. Huleatt had brought. That was not a book but a well known monthly magazine, an expensive one that cost two dollars a year. Caroline was privileged to have a neighbor who had such a periodical, and they had marvelous afternoons together, just visiting and looking at Godey's. They might have even talked about the necessity of Saturday night baths!

*"Another champion of the bathtub was Sarah Josepha Hale, the editor of America's foremost women's magazine, Godey's Lady's Book, who is credited with the spread of the Saturday night bath."*[63]

Can you see yourself visiting the Ingalls cabin in the big woods near Lund, Wisconsin?

You drop by unannounced, simply because there was very little way to announce yourself. Mary and Laura are out in the yard playing on the stumps, and they see you first.

"Ma, we have a visitor!"

Laura yelled that. Mary didn't yell.

In the door of the cabin steps a thin young lady, apron on, and she waves a few strands of hair from her damp forehead. Her hands smooth her apron self-consciously but her face breaks out into a genuine smile. She greets you as warmly as you have ever been greeted, and sends Laura running out to the field to tell Charles that they have a visitor. Charles walks back to the house briskly, shakes your hand vigorously while keeping a respectful distance, and inquires about your well-being. Also that of your family. Caroline says that she has midday dinner about ready and that you just must sit and eat with them. You smell the cooking, it smells good, but protest that you don't want to intrude. They all object that having dinner is no intrusion, and that they are glad to have your company.

So you join them in washing up at the pitcher and bowl and sitting down at the table. After thanks is given for the meal, the food is passed around, with you taking your helpings first. Caroline and Charles talk with you, not about what they want to talk about but whatever it is you want to talk about. They put you first. Then to your answers and comments they add their own, with great discretion and consideration. The food is warm, the room is warm, but most of all, the visit is warm. They like you and are glad to see you.

They are so glad you came.

And when you leave and walk away out of the sunlight and into the cool big woods, you know they meant it, and you're glad you came, too. You've had a pleasant visit with the Ingalls.

Modern transportation has enabled us today to visit often. Actually, we are almost always surrounded by people.

Constant crowds and modern gadgetry, though, may cause us to hardly visit at all, even when we are together.

In Laura's pioneer times, people were with other people much less often, but when they were, it was worth much more.

*Chapter 11 (Harvest)*

# Cousin Charley's Training

Charley did not want to fetch the water jug.

Laura did not care for cousin Charley's upbringing.

She wrote about him repeatedly. And when she wrote about him getting stung, her words had a little sting to them.

Laura wrote about Charley in her *Pioneer Girl* manuscript, in much the same terms as in the big woods book. But years before, Laura had written about Cousin Charley to her *Missouri Ruralist* readers, in an article published on June 5, 1919, soon after the First World War had ended.

*"After reading the staggering total of the indemnity demanded by the Allies from Germany and adding to that sum the amount of the country's internal war indebtedness, it is very plain to anyone that*

Germany is bankrupt, that it will take many, many years to pay these debts and make the credit of the country good once more.

But there is an even worse thing which has come upon Germany — the nation is morally bankrupt, also. No one has attempted to put a money value upon this failure, knowing that the honor of a nation, as of an individual, is beyond price, but it is sure that Germany will keep paying on this debt, which it owes the world, for many years, also probably for generations.

The first installment of this debt is being collected now and that it is hard for the nation to make the payment is shown by an interview with Germany's foreign minister, Brockdorff-Rantan, in which he says, "The peace terms are simply unbelievable, because they ask the impossible. The entente demands material guarantees and will not accept moral guarantees. This shows its distrust of us. We desire an organized world in which Germany will have the same rights as other people."

Germany is finding that as a nation which has for four years deliberately broken its pledged word, that word is of no value: that it is bankrupt in moral guarantees.

The entente is in the position, with Germany, of the hill man who fought another man for telling an untruth about him. He had knocked his enemy down and was still beating him tho he was crying "enough' when a stranger came along and interfered.

"Stop! Stop!" he exclaimed. "Don't you hear him hollering enough?"

"Oh, yes!" replied the hill man, but he is such a liar I don't know whether he is telling the truth or not."

When I was a girl at home, my father came in from the harvest field one day at noon and with great glee told what had befallen my cousin Charley. Father and Uncle Henry were harvesting a field of wheat in the old fashioned way, cutting it by hand with cradles and Charley, who was about 10 years old, followed them around the field for play. He lagged behind until the men were ahead of him and then began to scream, jumping up and down and throwing his arms around. Father and Uncle Henry dropped their cradles and ran to him thinking a snake had bitten him or that something in the woods close by was frightening him, but when they came to Charley he stopped screaming and laughed at them.

Charley fooled them this way three times, but they grew tired and warm and had been deceived so many times that when for the fourth time he began to scream they looked back at him as he jumped up and down, then turned away and went on with their work.

But Charley kept on screaming and there seemed to be a new note in his voice, so finally they walked back to where he was and found that he was in a yellow jackets' nest and the more he jumped and threw his arms and screamed the more came to sting him.

"I'd like to have the training of that young man for a little while," said father, "but I don't believe I could have thought of a better way to punish him for his meanness."

Boys or men or nations it seems to be the same, if they prove themselves liars times enough, nobody will believe them when they do tell the truth.

"Getting down to first causes, what makes one nation choose the high way and another nation choose the low way? What produces character and conscience in a nation, anyhow? What produces the *other thing?" asks a writer in an article in the Saturday Evening Post? And the question is left unanswered.*

*In a country ruled as Germany has been there is no doubt the character of the nation received the impress of the rulers, coming from them down to the people. In a country such as ours, the national character is also like that of the rulers, but in this case the rulers are the people and it is they who impress themselves upon it. The character of each individual one of us affects our national character for good or bad.*

*Training! School training: home training: mother's training! And there you are back to the first causes in the making of an honorable, truthful, upright individual, the kind of citizens who collectively make an honorable, treaty-keeping nation, a nation that chooses the high way instead of the low."*

Did you notice what Pa said?

*"I'd like to have the training of that young man for a little while," said father, "but I don't believe I could have thought of a better way to punish him for his meanness."*

He didn't care for Charley's upbringing, either!

Rural people of that time knew and tried to follow these proverbs. Remember in that America, if a family had only one book, and most had few more than that, it was a Bible.

Proverbs 22 (KJV)
(6) Train up a child in the way he should go: and when he is old, he will not depart from it.

Proverbs 29 (KJV)

(17) Correct thy son, and he shall give thee rest; yea, he shall give delight unto thy soul.

Proverbs 22 (KJV)

(15) Foolishness is bound in the heart of a child; but the rod of correction shall drive it far from him.

Indeed, children of that time were more respectful of others and did give their parents 'rest', compared to later versions of American youth. But Charley had not been raised according to those proverbs; that is, he had not been made to obey his parents or be respectful of other people. Charley was the son of Aunt Polly, Charles' younger sister, and Uncle Henry Quiner, Caroline's older brother. They're the couple who jointly bought the 160 acres with Caroline and Charles. But Aunt Polly and Uncle Henry had different ideas about raising children than Caroline and Charles and Laura.

Charley pretended to be hurt and wasn't. Pa said that was a lie. But Charley went farther than just breaking the commandment, 'thou shalt not bear false witness.'

Rain threatened to ruin Uncle Henry's crop. If they lost the grain crop, they lost much of Henry's work for the year, making life even harder for Aunt Polly and Charley and the other children in the family. Henry and Charles were working feverishly to harvest the grain before rain came. That did not mean that they were driving tractors around the field. It did not even mean that they were driving teams of horses around the field pulling harvesting machines. It meant they were cutting the whole field of grain – by hand.

They used scythes with cradles. Webster's 1828 dictionary says that the cradle is *"a frame of wood, with long bending teeth, to which is fastened a scythe, for cutting and laying oats and other grain in a swath."* That tool by itself sounds heavy. The scythe has a long curved handle and a fairly heavy blade, and when a wooden cradle is fastened on, it makes for a heavy tool, especially when a swath of grain is laid on the cradle, and is swung all day long.

An article about threshing points out how exhausting it was to harvest grains by hand.

*"The annual harvest of "small grains"—wheat, oats, rye, and barley—was not taken lightly by our farming forefathers. Not only were grain crops able to be sold for cash, but they were required for use as food, animal fodder, and the ingredients for salable items from bread to whiskey.*

*The problem with the harvest was its labor-intensive character. Small grains ripen during the hottest months of the summer and the harvest required cutting acres of tough stalks with hand sickles or scythes, hours spent bundling the stalks and then stacking them in shocks to dry, and then later beating the bundles with flails to separate the grain from the hulls and stalks before winnowing it to remove the chaff."*[64]

The key to using a scythe is to let the tool swing itself. The user gets in a rhythm and swings the scythe back and forward, using the weight of the blade as a pendulum, not trying to force it with the arms and keeping the muscles taut, but letting the arms swing loosely with the tool. Using it like that, the cutter can swing over and over, back and forth for a long time, because the muscles are not tense and clenched.

However, human muscles do get tired. Henry and Charles were cutting in that field for hour after hour, from sunup until dinnertime at midday. They feared they weren't going to beat the rain, so Henry told Charley to come to the field with them.

Charley was almost eleven years old, according to the big woods book. Today that doesn't seem very old, but back then, when young children were taught to be very responsible, eleven was plenty old enough to work and help the family stay alive. Pa Ingalls and Almanzo both had driven horses in the field when they were only nine years old. Not only were they able to physically do the work, but at that young age they had the character and responsibility to do the work. In the "Wonderful Machine" chapter, little girl Laura used a knife to cut up the pumpkin and she stood on a chair to stir the hot pumpkin, even though she was a tiny girl. Almost no parent would allow a child to do those jobs today. And in the "Sundays" chapter, Laura mentioned that, at age five, she was knitting Carrie a pair of mittens, and at age seven, Mary was making a patchwork quilt.

So eleven-year-old Charley should surely be able to get a jug of water!

No, Charley wasn't going to swing a scythe or gather up the grain. All Charley had to do was to get water when the men needed it and fetch the whetstone for them. That wasn't like real work. By that time of the day, Henry and Charles were very tired and every step that Charley could save them was helpful, so by doing those little jobs, he could be a real help to his father and uncle.

But Charley didn't think about his father and his uncle or his mother and siblings, who depended on that crop. Charley only thought about himself.

First of all, he got in their way when they were trying to cut. That was dangerous for Charley, as disobedience to parents often is. Next, instead of fetching the whetstone so they could sharpen their scythes, he hid it.

Uncle Charles must have thought that was really funny.

What's more, when those hot, thirsty men wanted a drink of water, maybe every hour or so, Charley didn't want to take them the jug. He wanted them to get their own water; he was busy.

Laura and Mary were horrified at Charley's impudence.

*"Then they heard Pa tell about what Charley had done. Laura and Mary were horrified. They were often naughty, themselves, but they had never imagined that anyone could be as naughty as Charley had been. He hadn't worked to help save the oats. He hadn't minded his father quickly when his father spoke to him. He had bothered Pa and Uncle Henry when they were hard at work."*[65]

In all of that, Charley did not think of anyone but himself. He had no compassion at all for the suffering. He only added to their suffering.

Then he had to suffer. His suffering did not come at the hand of his parents. It came at the hand of life. As Pa or Ma Ingalls might have said, 'what goes around comes around.'

Charley's parents probably thought they were loving him more than Caroline and Charles loved Mary and Laura. Laura was spanked for slapping Mary, but Charley was never made to stop disrespecting others.

However, Charley's parents nearly killed him.

When they did not teach him to control himself, his lack of self-control nearly did his self in. After pretending that he had a problem and fooling Henry and Charles several times, when Charley did have a real problem, they did not come to help him. Also, it must be observed that eleven-year-old Charley did not have enough personal responsibility – *common sense* – to know to run away from the bees, instead of just jumping up and down by their nest.

As Charles said, Charley had been 'spoiled.' His parents did not expect much of him, and that's what they got.

On the other hand, Caroline and Charles took great pains to teach their children character.

When Charles was smoking the deer, he told Laura to fetch him some hickory wood chips. Presto! She did it. She did not have to be told several times. She did not argue. She did not ask Pa why he needed stupid wood chips, anyway. Laura just went and fetched the wood chips.

The result of her obedience is that she was an asset to her family. In her little way, even at her young age, she helped to smoke the deer that the family ate in the winter.

When Pa was telling Mary and Laura the story of the big and little cats, Mary made a comment but Laura interrupted her.

Pa paused the story to instruct Laura that she should not interrupt people. In the story of "Pa and the Screech Owl," when little Charles Ingalls was tardy in getting the cows, the lesson was that children should obey their parents and they wouldn't be scared by screech owls. When Laura got her rag doll for Christmas, Ma wanted her to share the doll with the other girls and instructed her that little girls should not be selfish. Ma and Laura were in great danger when Ma thought a bear was their cow. Ma told Laura to walk back to the house: not run to the house, not wait five minutes and then go to the house, but just *walk to the house*. Because Laura had been taught to obey, she saved herself a bear of a time.

You see, a great part of the time, Ma and Pa were actively teaching their girls how to treat people. But Charley had not been taught that by his parents, and because of their lack of teaching, he got in trouble. By not teaching him to respect others, they had taught him to always put himself first. Around their home, then, they would not have had peace, as the Ingalls did. Charley would have been just like he was when he was in the field, and their other kids may have been the same way. Each kid who tried to put himself first clashed with all the others who did the same. Instead of peace, that makes for constant bickering and jousting, with each person trying to get his own way.

We remember the Ingalls most for their evenings around the fire, with Pa playing the fiddle. What if Charley had been there in their home? Would he have torn Laura's paper dolls, hid Pa's fiddle bow or stuck Ma with a mending needle?

The Ingalls family evenings around the fire weren't wonderful just because of the fire and fiddle, but because of the love and respect that each member of the family had for all others. That love and respect was no accident. That was how the girls were taught.

*"Mrs. Peterson talked Swedish to them, and they talked English to her, and they understood each other perfectly. She always gave them each a cookie when they left, and they nibbled the cookies very slowly while they walked home.*

*Laura nibbled away exactly half of hers, and Mary nibbled exactly half of hers, and the other halves they saved for Baby Carrie. Then when they got home, Carrie had two halfcookies, and that was a whole cookie.*

*This wasn't right. All they wanted to do was to divide the cookies fairly with Carrie. Still, if Mary saved half her cookie, while Laura ate the whole of hers, or if Laura saved half, and Mary ate her whole cookie, that wouldn't be fair, either.*

*They didn't know what to do. So each saved half, and gave it to Baby Carrie. But they always felt that somehow that wasn't quite fair."*

Without being told to, both girls saved half a cookie for baby sister Carrie. They wanted to divide the cookies evenly, but their math was still undeveloped. Most of all, though, they wanted to share, as they had been taught, and that attitude had developed well.

## Chapter 12 (Wonderful Machine)

# Threshing the Grain, Thrashing through Life

Threshing Grain by Thrashing

Pa had threshed his wheat the way people did in Bible times.

To thresh wheat is to beat it. Threshing and thrashing are variants from the same root with the same basic meaning: to beat. Thrashing was often used as 'give you a thrashing.'

When little Charles didn't mind his pa and bring the cows straight home, then Grandpa *"gave me a good thrashing, so that I would remember to mind him after that."*

So people thrashed the wheat, or beat it, or threshed it. Up until the new machine came in, Pa threshed his wheat in much the same way as had been done for thousands of years.

In the Bible, King David once sinned by counting how big his army was, causing a plague on Israel. The plague stopped at a threshing floor.

> 1 Chronicles 21 (WEB)
> (13) David said to Gad, I am in distress. Let me fall, I pray, into the hand of Yahweh; for very great are his mercies: and let me not fall into the hand of man.
> (14) So Yahweh sent a pestilence on Israel; and there fell of Israel seventy thousand men.
> (15) God sent an angel to Jerusalem to destroy it: and as he was about to destroy, Yahweh saw, and he relented of the disaster, and said to the destroying angel, It is enough; now stay your hand. The angel of Yahweh was standing by the threshing floor of Ornan the Jebusite.

Ornan and his sons were threshing wheat as all this was going on. When the angel of God appeared, that really must have broken up the monotony of everyday threshing. David then built an altar at Ornan's threshing floor. His threshing floor became the site of the temple that Solomon built, on the temple mount in Jerusalem, that has been the focus of world history ever since.

2 Chronicles 3 (WEB)

(1) Then Solomon began to build the house of Yahweh at Jerusalem on Mount Moriah, where Yahweh appeared to David his father, which he made ready in the place that David had appointed, in the threshing floor of Ornan the Jebusite.

An encyclopedia explains threshing in more modern terms.

*"[T]hreshing or thrashing, separation of grain from the stalk on which it grows and from the chaff or pod that covers it. The first known method was by striking the reaped ears of grain with a flail. In another early method horses or oxen trod out the grain from stalks spread on a threshing floor. In both cases the straw was raked away and then the mixture of grain and chaff was winnowed, i.e., tossed into or poured through a current of air so that the light chaff was blown away from the heavier grain."*[66]

That was basically the same process that Ornan and his boys used.

In more recent times, a doctor turned teacher grew a little wheat in his backyard near Newark, New Jersey. Then, of course, he had to thresh it.

*"[A]ny farmer back in Biblical times knew that wheat did not come in two parts. The chaff is an integral part of the wheat plant, the dry husk surrounding the wheat berry, the part used for food.*

*Before winnowing the chaff from the wheat berries, you need to thresh the wheat. Threshing is basically knocking the wheat kernels off the rest of the plant. Today this is done with a combination reaper/thresher (called combine for short), a machine that can cost well over a million dollars.*

*I was not going to invest a million dollars to harvest a tiny patch of wheat. I got to do it the old-fashioned way--beating the wheat until my arms were ready to fall off.*

*Initially I tried a Wiffle ball bat. Little success.*

*I made a flail--two sticks tied together end-to-end, allowing me to beat the heads of wheat much more efficiently...*

*Flailing is very hard work. I pounded and pounded my small stook, (a number of sheaves set upright in a field to dry with their heads together.[67]) I once shoveled scrap metal on ships in Port Newark. I'm not sure which is harder.*

*The chaff is an integral part of the plant, not some sinister fluff stalking the grain...*

*Before separating a part from itself, you need to break it. Threshing wheat requires violence. The wheat plant is broken...*

*Indeed, the actual separating part is easy. Once the grain is threshed, just wait for a breezy day and toss the threshed grain in the air. The wheat berries will bounce at your feet, the chaff blown away. People once knew this. Wheat and chaff were not distinct elements until after the threshing...*

*I will not likely grow wheat again; I have too little land, and the work of threshing by hand is a bit much for a man in his sixth decade.*

*What do I have to show for it? Well, I have a half pint of homegrown wheat sitting in a Mason jar, enough for a couple of bagels should I grind it into flour.*

More importantly, I have a better grasp of "separating the wheat from the chaff," and what a loaf of bread meant to my forebears, and still means to most of the people alive today."[68]

Surprisingly, by the time Pa Ingalls used a threshing machine, such machines had been around for nearly a century, as the encyclopedia article further explains.

"In 1784 a Scotsman, Andrew Meikle, devised a threshing machine. Sheaves of grain were fed into a revolving cylinder armed with wooden beaters. Another toothed drum raked away the loose straw and pushed the remaining chaff and grain through a sieve onto a series of rollers that further separated the chaff from the grain in preparation for winnowing. The principle of Meikle's machine has been retained in all threshing machines up to and including the modern self-propelled combines. [A] combine [is an] agricultural machine that performs both harvesting and threshing operations. Although it was not widely used until the 1930s, the combine was in existence as early as 1830."

The 1881 Household Cyclopedia said of Meikle's machine:

"Since the invention of this machine, Mr. Meikle and others have progressively introduced a variety of improvements, all tending to simplify the labour, and to augment the quantity of the work performed. When first erected, though the grain was equally well separated from the straw, yet as the whole of the straw, chaff, and grain, was indiscriminately thrown into a confused heap, the work could only with propriety be considered as half executed. By the addition of rakes, or shakers, and two pairs of fanners, all driven by the same machinery, the different processes of thrashing, shaking, and winnowing are now all at once performed, and the grain immediately prepared for the public market. When it is added, that *the quantity of grain gained from the superior powers of the machine is fully equal to a twentieth part of the crop, and that, in some cases, the expense of thrashing and cleaning the grain is considerably less than what was formerly paid for cleaning it alone, the immense saving arising from the invention will at once be seen."*

Pa had to pay for the use of the eight-horsepower threshing machine with part of his wheat, but the machine was so efficient that Pa came out with more wheat than he would have if he had done all his threshing by hand.

*"That machine's a great invention!"* [Pa] *said. "Other folks can stick to old-fashioned ways if they want to, but I'm all for progress. It's a great age we're living in. As long as I raise wheat, I'm going to have a machine come and thresh it, if there's one anywhere in the neighborhood."*[69]

Pa Ingalls finally got a break. He saved two weeks of back-breaking work and wound up with more wheat. No wonder he was so pleased with that machine!

Charles and Caroline had a tough life on the frontier.

They were married on February 1, 1860. Caroline was twenty years old and Charles was twenty-four.[70] Only a year later, the American Civil War began and Charles was of prime soldiering age. Charles had two brothers who served in the Union Army, Caroline lost a brother on the Union side at the Battle of Shiloh in 1862,[71] and tens of thousands of Wisconsin men joined them in the war, but Charles did not.

Instead, in the middle of the war, he bought a farm, as a biographer of Laura describes.

*"On September 22, 1863, Charles teamed up with Caroline's brother Henry to purchase a quarter-section of land from an Englishman named Charles Nunn, who worked as a druggist in the village of Reed's Landing on the other side of Lake Pepin. They paid him $335 for the property, advancing only $35 in cash and taking out a mortgage on the rest. The parcel was on high ground, seven miles mainly north and a little west of Pepin. It was largely covered with trees but also contained some clearings where they could begin planting crops. Henry agreed to work the north eighty acres, with Charles taking the south half of the property."[72]*

The whole farm cost $335, but there was no way that Charles and Henry could come up with that kind of money. However, by pooling their savings they came up with $35.

$35!

Think of what that meant to Charles and Caroline. By saving bits of his wages for two years – less than two dimes per week – Charles and Caroline were able to scrape together $17.50. Then by combining theirs with Henry and Polly's money, they made a $35 down payment on a farm, financed the other $300, and each family had 80 acres of land to farm.

How twenty-six year old Pa and twenty-two year old Ma must have felt when they bought that farm – *their farm!*

But their farm had many trees. Those trees did produce some harvest. In the fall, they gathered walnuts, hazelnuts and hickory nuts, and Pa hunted in those woods for meat. Charles used those trees to build his log home, the little house in the big woods. And those trees built the barn and the rail fence around the barn. But forests don't grow corn and wheat to sell.

Charles and Caroline did not begin their family until the Civil War was almost over. Their first baby, Mary, was born on January 10, 1865, close to the end of the war in April when Lee surrendered to Grant at Appomattox. Laura was born two years later in 1867 and Carrie came along in 1870.

So at the time that Laura remembered in the big woods, Caroline and Charles had been married for about a decade and had three children, all girls, and their own little farm with a big mortgage on it. Their farm had many trees, and the open land was always sprouting new little trees, to try to take back what had been taken from the forest. Clearing new farmland from the big woods was difficult, time-consuming work. Caroline was just over thirty years old by then and Charles was already in his mid-thirties when they had that wheat crop to harvest. It couldn't have been much of a wheat crop, because it takes a lot of land to grow a lot of wheat, but it was something.

And when they had the threshers there to thresh their wheat, don't you know that was a big day for Caroline and Charles!

Caroline had to cook for the whole crew, no small task and no small amount of food. When Laura did the same thing as a new wife more than a decade later, she mistakenly left the sugar out of the rhubarb pie. Rhubarb is about as sour as sour can be, so the workers just lifted the top crust of the pie and poured the sugar in. The first man who tasted that sugarless rhubarb pie, though, may have gone to his grave with a slight pucker.

Caroline had no such catastrophes when she served the threshing crew. She was still a young woman, with a house full of little girls, yet she always seemed so mature. She wanted to feed the crew well, because that wheat crop meant so much to them, but she had to work very hard. Caroline did not complain, she taught her daughters that they must never complain, and when they did, she reminded them not to. Even though she did not complain, her work was extremely difficult as a pioneer wife on the frontier.

In fact, Laura almost refused to marry Almanzo because of Caroline's hard work. Just before she was married, Laura decided she didn't want to marry a farmer.

*"Laura twisted the bright gold ring with its pearl-and-garnet setting around and around on the forefinger of her left hand. It was a pretty ring and she liked having it, but... "I've been thinking," she said. "I don't want to marry a farmer. I have always said I never would. I do wish you would do something else. There are chances in town now while it is so new and growing."*

*Again there was a little silence; then Manly asked, "Why don't you want to marry a farmer?"*

*And Laura replied, "Because a farm is such a hard place for a woman. There are so many chores for her to do, and harvest help and threshers to cook for."*[73]

Caroline's work was not easy, almost *complain*-able. Laura had seen that and did not want to live it herself.

It goes without saying that Charles also had a great burden of tiresome work, even with the new eight-horsepower threshing machine. He didn't complain a lot, either.

Caroline and Charles were just a young couple, with a young family, a farm full of trees, and no money. They had saved up

$17.50 to buy their farm and they were putting their all into it. They were threshing their grain and thrashing through life, just trying to make it, like so many other couples throughout history, before that time, at that time, since that time.

And while they were struggling through life, they were happy.

Through the years, Ma and Pa Ingalls had a lot of crops that failed. But that year, in the big woods, they had a wheat crop, they threshed it with a machine, they fed all the threshers and they thanked God for all their blessings.

Can you see them as the threshing machine was pulled on down the road, standing in front of their little gray log cabin, Ma holding Carrie, Mary and Laura at her skirts, and Pa's wiry hair waving in the breeze, surrounded by the tall trees of the big woods?

Caroline and Charles were just trying to make it, threshing the wheat and thrashing through life.

*Chapter 13 (Deer in the Wood)*

# Big Woods, Little Cabin, Huge Love

Ingalls family love stretches through the pages
and on through the years.

Today there are no big woods at the Ingalls farmstead. Most of the trees are gone.

Pa was afraid that the sprouts would take back his farmland.

*"Those sprouts are getting waist-high around the stumps in the wheat-field. A man just has to keep everlasting at it, or the woods'll take back the place."*[74]

The sprouts did not win out; the farmers did. When Pa left to farm somewhere else, other farmers moved in, at his place and all around it. Today the area is filled with beautiful farms of all types.

If the Ingalls were to take their wagon down the road to Pepin today, they would pass croplands growing grains, as Pa did on his field. They would pass grassy pastures filled with dairy cows, where farmers decided the land was better suited for grass than grains. And they would pass trees, stands of forest that have not been cleared for crops, a remainder and reminder of the big woods that went on for as far as a man could walk in a day, a week or a month.

Surely at some point in their travels in Pepin, the Ingalls passed by where the Laura Ingalls Wilder Museum is today.

*"The Laura Ingalls Wilder Memorial Society, Inc., was officially organized in July of 1974. Through the generosity of the Pepin business community and the present landowner, the society was fortunate in acquiring three acres of land at the original site of Laura's birth.*

*The museum is open 10 a.m. - 5 p.m. from May 15th through October 15th, then Friday, Saturday and Sunday until October 27th. We are closed over the winter season. We're conveniently located on the Great River Road."*

That three acres the Laura Ingalls Wilder Memorial Society acquired became the Little House Wayside, seven miles north of Pepin and about a mile southeast of Lund, although Lund is just a few houses at the junction of county roads CC and J. The Little House Wayside has a replica of the Ingalls log cabin and the surrounding countryside is mostly farmland, not forest. The yard around the cabin, where Laura and Mary used to play on the stumps, is dotted with a number of trees, but the land is mostly a well-kept, grassy lawn.

Even though the Ingalls farm site is no longer in the big woods, the big woods are still in Wisconsin.

In Laura's time, forests covered about three-fourths of Wisconsin, and a great timber industry came from that. Today, forests still cover about half the state and the big woods are now expanding. Every year the sprouts take over a little more of Wisconsin's land, but only because people want them to.

Actually, such a mix makes for a lovely blend, with grains waving in the breeze, verdant grasslands dotted with black and white cows, and rich forests covering the least usable land. Pa Ingalls would probably be quite pleased.

At the Ingalls' farmstead, in the last chapter of Laura's book about the big woods, freezing nights had come again, as at the beginning of the book. Again the family had put away food for the winter, and again they spent slow evenings together by the fire. Their family was almost always together, in time and in spirit.

The Ingalls had a family enterprise.

What was their family enterprise?

Staying alive.

That's right. Just staying alive was the family enterprise. Together they worked diligently at that.

They did not pursue their enterprise for fame or riches or career aspirations. They worked as hard as they could and as long as they could because that's what it took just to stay alive.

It's almost impossible for people today to realize the way life was for most people before the twentieth century. Rose Wilder Lane did realize that and in the early 1940's wrote about it in her direct style.

*"But surely, men have always wanted enough to eat. Yet for six thousand years most men have been hungry. Many of them have always been dying of hunger...*

*For sixty known centuries, multitudes of men have lived on this earth. Their situation has been the everlasting human situation. Their desire to live has been as strong as ours. Their energy has always been enough to make this earth at least habitable for human beings. Their intelligence has been great.*

*Yet for six thousand years, most men have been hungry. Famines have always killed multitudes, and still do over most of this earth. Ninety-five years ago [from 1943], the Irish were starving to death; no one was surprised. Europeans had never expected to get from this earth enough food to keep them all alive."*[75]

Caroline, Charles, Mary and Laura were a team. They were in the battle of life together. Anyone who thought only of himself or herself hurt all the others. The family came before the self and the good of all was more important than the wants of any one.

Therefore each person did what he or she could do best. Ma didn't hunt bears or wrestle the plow in the field. Pa did that.

Although some women did plow at times, out of necessity, Charles was much better at such physical things than Caroline was. Pa didn't make rag dolls or mold butter with a lovely strawberry on top. He could have done those things, but Caroline was much better at them than Charles was, and Pa probably would never have colored the butter with grated carrot. The girls picked up wood chips, washed their own dishes, and made their own beds. Those were jobs they could do, even at a young age. As they got older, then they were able to do other jobs. Laura even helped with the haying, just before the long winter, because that was what was needed at the time.

All did what they could do best and all did all they could do. When everyone did that, the family became more than the sum of its parts. By working together and going in the same direction, they went farther than if they had spread out in four directions.

Most of all, by each putting the others before the self in the battle to keep them all alive, they became a family. They were not just a family in name, because they were biologically related. They were a family in fact, united with a kinship that went beyond blood. Their family was always together, raising food, preserving food, eating together and enjoying the food, riding the wagon together in the stillness of the woods, and sitting around the fire together in the evenings. Caroline, Charles, Mary, Laura and Carrie were always together.

In *These Happy Golden Years*, when Laura first left her home to teach school, she stayed with a family that wasn't really a family, the way the Ingalls were. While living in that dreadful house, Laura wrote of how she dreamed of home.

*"Then Pa came driving from town on the bobsled; he called to Laura, "How about going home for Saturday, Half-Pint?" Ma and Mary and Carrie and Grace were so surprised! Mary said happily, "Oh, Laura!" Ma's whole face lighted with her smiling. Carrie hurried to help Laura take off her wraps, and Grace jumped up and down, clapping her hands. "Charles, why didn't you tell us!" Ma said, and Pa answered, "Why, Caroline, I said I'd do a little hauling. Laura's little." And Laura remembered how, at the dinner table, Pa had drunk his tea and pushed back his cup and said, "Guess I'll do a little hauling this afternoon." Ma said, "Oh, Charles!" Laura had not gone away from home at all; she was there."*[76]

But that was all just a dream.

Notice that Laura did not dream about the house. Goodness knows she lived in too many little houses to dream about. When she dreamed about home, she dreamed about her family.

When gray haired Laura wrote about *Little House in the Big Woods*, sixty years had passed from the time she had lived that story. In the book, Laura told us how they smoked deer and made headcheese, tapped maple syrup and danced at Grandpa's, and traveled through the woods and saw Lake Pepin. But most of all, Laura told us about her family. Her words told us how they did things, but her spirit showed us how they loved each other.

The ending of *Little House in the Big Woods* is well known. This was read by the Laura character in the television series *Little House: A New Beginning*, episode "Once Upon A Time."

*"She [Laura] looked at Ma gently rocking and knitting. She thought to herself, 'This is now.' She was glad that the cozy house, and Pa,*

and Ma, and the firelight, and the music, was now. It could not be forgotten, she thought, because now is now. It can never be a long time ago."

'Now' always becomes long ago, and it always does so sooner than we think it will. But there are some things that never change, some values that always endure, some laws that are perpetual, throughout all time and in any century.

Laura wrote, ""There is nothing new under the sun," says the proverb. I think the meaning is that there are just so many truths or laws of life and no matter how far we may think we have advanced we cannot get beyond those laws. However complex a structure we build of living we must come back to those truths and so we find we have traveled in a circle."

One of those enduring values is family love. When Pa fiddled by the firelight while Ma knitted by the hearth, they created much more than music. They created family – a loving family, a bond that included biology but went far beyond it, with a love strong enough to stretch through the pages of Laura's books, and then on down through the years, decades, and centuries.

Even reaching down to us.

# ENDNOTES

[1] New World Encyclopedia, "Laura Ingalls Wilder," http://www.newworld encyclopedia.org/entry/Laura_Ingalls_Wilder.

[2] Laura Ingalls Wilder, *Missouri Ruralist*, February 20, 1918.

[3] Wisconsin Historical Society, "Laura Ingalls Wilder," http://www. wisconsinhistory.org/topics/wilder/.

[4] Laura Ingalls Wilder, *Missouri Ruralist*, March 5, 1916.

[5] Department of Natural Resources, *Wisconsin*, "Appendix B: Cultural History of Wisconsin's Forests," http://dnr.wi.gov/topic/forestplanning/ documents/appendixb_100721.pdf.

[6] Sarah Biondich, "The Great Peshtigo Fire," ExpressMilwaukee.com, June 9,2010, http://expressmilwaukee.com/article-11172-the-great-peshtigo-fire.html.

[7] Rose Wilder Lane, *Old Home Town*, (Lincoln: University of Nebraska, 1963), chapter I.

[8] Anne Elizabeth Baker, *Glossary of Northamptonshire Words and Phrases*, (London: J.R. Smith Publishers, 1854).

[9] Kerri McIntire, *The Almanack: the Inheritage Journal of History, Travel and Lore*, "Mother Goose Migrates to America," 2000, http://www.inheritage. org/almanack/b_goose.html.

[10] Laura Ingalls Wilder, *Missouri Ruralist*, June 28, 1913.

[11] Ibid, September 5, 1916.

[12] Ibid, September 20, 1916.

[13] Rose Wilder Lane, *The Discovery of Freedom*, (Baltimore: Laissez Faire Books, 2012), chapter The Third Attempt.

[14] Laura Ingalls Wilder, *Missouri Ruralist*, April 20, 1917,

[15] Ibid, September 1, 1921.

[16] Ibid, September 15, 1921.

[17] Ibid, June 1, 1924.

[18] "The Rifle versus the Musket," *The History of American Technology*, 1998, http://web.bryant.edu/~ehu/h364/materials/musket/rev_gun5.htm.

[19] Janet Benge and Geoff Benge, *Laura Ingalls Wilder, A Storybook Life*, (Lynwood, WA: Emerald Books, 2005.

[20] Meghan Clyne, "Lessons in Liberty from Laura Ingalls Wilder," *National Affairs*, issue 12, summer 2012, http://www.nationalaffairs.com/publications/detail/lessons-in-liberty-from-laura-ingalls-wilder.

[21] Abraham Lincoln, *Brainy Quotes*, http://www.brainyquote.com/quotes/quotes/a/abrahamlin109275.html.

[22] Rose Wilder Lane, *Old Home Town*, chapter I.

[23] http://www.wisegeek.org/what-does-throwing-the-baby-out-with-the-bath-water-mean.htm.

[24] Kelsey Freeman, "English Victorian Society," Trafton Academy, English, Dec. 13.1997, http://kspot.org/holmes/kelsey.htm.

[25] William Shakespeare, *Romeo and Juliet*, Act II, Scene I.

[26] Edwards Park, "To Bathe or Not to Bathe: Coming Clean in Colonial America," *Colonial Williamsburg Journal*, Autumn 2000, http://www.history.org/foundation/journal/autumn00/bathe.cfm.

[27] Katherine Ashenburg, *The Dirt on Clean: An Unsanitized History*, (New York: North Point Press, 2008), p 188.

[28] Edwards Park, "To Bathe or Not to Bathe."

[29] "Etiquette and Manners: Victorian Era," *The Old Farmer's Almanac*, http://www.almanac.com/content/etiquette-and-manners-victorian-era.

[30] Edwards Park, "To Bathe or Not to Bathe."

[31] *Gleanings from Our Past, A History of the Iowa Braille and Sight Saving School*, Vinton School for the Blind, Vinton Iowa, pgs. 23-29, published by The Iowa Braille & Sight Saving School 1984 APH Museum: Mary Ingalls Online Exhibit, http://www.aph.org/museum/MaryIowa.html.

[32] Laura Ingalls Wilder, *Missouri Ruralist*, March 20, 1916.

[33] Rose Wilder Lane, *Old Home Town*, chapter I.

[34] Ibid, chapter IX.

[35] Jules Verne, *Hier et demain (Yesterday and Tomorrow) A collection of short stories*, 1910, http://epguides.com/djk/julesverne/works.shtml.

[36] Henry Grady Weaver, *The Mainspring of Human Progress*, (Talbot Books: 1947), (Revised edition Foundation for Economic Education, Inc.:1953).

[37] Rose Wilder Lane, *Give Me Liberty*, first published in 1936, chapter XII.

[38] Ibid.

[39] Ibid.

[40] Laura Ingalls Wilder, *Missouri Ruralist*, February 5, 1920.

[41] Interview with Dean Butler, December 8, 2007, PrairieFans.com, http://www.pioneerontheprairie.com/dean.htm.

[42] Meghan Clyne, "Lessons in Liberty from Laura Ingalls Wilder."

[43] Ibid.

[44] Carla Killough McClafferty, *The Many Faces of George Washington: Remaking a Presidential Icon*, (Carolrhoda Books: 2013), chapter Becoming George Washington.

[45] Kate Van Winkle Keller and Charles Cyril Hendrickson, "George Washington and the Dance," http://www.colonialmusic.org/.

[46] "Delaine," *Encyclopedia Britannica*, http://www.britannica.com/EBchecked/topic/156299/delaine.

[47] Robert B. Thomas, , "Ma Ingalls' `delaine' was a party dress," *Deseret News*, Sunday, Dec. 28 1997, http://www.deseretnews.com/article/603346/Ma-Ingalls-delaine-was-a-party-dress.html?pg=all.

[48] Martyn Gorman, "Fashionable Clothing," University of Aberdeen, Department of Zoology, 2002, http://www.scran.ac.uk/packs/exhibitions/learning_materials/webs/40/fashion.htm.

[49] "Fiddle," http://www.thefreedictionary.com/fiddle.

[50] "Country Dance," http://www.britannica.com/EBchecked/topic/140377/country-dance.

[51] Rebecca Jones, "Everyone Dances from the angels on down," *Contra Conversations*, #1, March 8, 2001, http://www.neohiocontradance.org/html/history.html.

[52] Laura Ingalls Wilder, *Little House in the Big Woods*, HarperCollins Publishers, chapter "Dance at Grandpa's."

[53] Free Dictionary, "Go to town," http://idioms.thefreedictionary.com/go+to+town.

[54] Rose Wilder Lane, *The Discovery of Freedom*, p 228.

[55] http://www.hmdb.org/marker.asp?marker=45700

[56] http://www.explorewisconsin.com/spotlight/pepincounty

[57] http://www.hmdb.org/marker.asp?marker=45308

[58] Pierce County Historical Association, 1850-1900, http://www.piercecountyhistorical.org/18501900.php.

[59] The Historical Marker Data Base, Swedish Methodist Church, http://www.hmdb.org/marker.asp?marker=39752.

[60] Alan H. Winquist and Jessica Rousselow-Winquist, Touring *Swedish America, Where to Go and What to See*, (St. Paul: Minnesota Historical Society Press, 2006), p 132.

[61] Laura Ingalls Wilder, *Missouri Ruralist*, January 5, 1917.

[62] Laura Ingalls Wilder, *Pioneer Girl*, the unpublished first manuscript Laura submitted.

[63] Katherine Ashenburg, *The Dirt on Clean: An Unsanitized History*, p 107.

[64] "When threshing machines were harvest kings," *Oswego, Illinois Ledger-Sentinel*, 8/2/2007, http://www.ledgersentinel.com/default.asp.

[65] Laura Ingalls Wilder, *Little House in the Big Woods*, chapter "Harvest."

[66] http://encyclopedia2.thefreedictionary.com/threshing.

[67] http://www.collinsdictionary.com/dictionary/english/stook?show CookiePolicy=true

[68] Doyle, *Science Teacher blog spot*, "Separating Wheat from Chaff," http://doyle-scienceteach.blogspot.com/2009/03/separating-wheat-from-chaff.html.

[69] Laura Ingalls Wilder, *Little House in the Big Woods*, chapter "Wonderful Machine."

[70] Born Jan 1836 to married Feb 1860 = 24 years old.

[71] John E. Miller, *Becoming Laura Ingalls Wilder*, (Columbia, MO: University of Missouri Press, 1999), chapter 1.

[72] Ibid.

[73] Laura Ingalls Wilder, *The First Four Years*, HarperCollins Publishers, chapter "The First Year."

[74] Laura Ingalls Wilder, *Little House in the Big Woods*, chapter "Summertime."

[75] Rose Wilder Lane, *Discovery of Freedom*, originally published in 1943 by John Day Company, NY, chapter "Situation."

[76] Laura Ingalls Wilder, *These Happy Golden Years*, HarperCollins Publishing, chapter "Laura Leaves Home."

# Other books by Dan L. White

Information available at danlwhitebooks.com
Email at mail@danlwhitebooks.com.
Find us on Facebook.

## Laura Ingalls' Friends Remember Her
*Memories from Laura's Ozark Home*

– contains memories from Laura and Almanzo's close friends, Ozarkers who knew them around their home town of Mansfield, Missouri. We chat with these folks, down home and close up, about their good friends Laura and Almanzo.

Laura also joins in our chats because we include long swatches of her magazine writings on whatever subject is at hand. It's almost as if she's there talking with us. Her thoughts on family and little farms and what-not are more interesting than almost anybody you've ever talked to.

Plus the book contains discussions of –
  * how Laura's Ozark life made her happy books possible;
  * what made Laura's books so happy;
  * whether her daughter Rose wrote Laura's books;
  * and Laura's last, lonely little house.

*Laura Ingalls' Friends Remember Her* includes -
  * her friends' recollections;
  * Laura's writings from her magazine articles;
  * and fresh discussions of Laura's happy books and her life.

Laura's readers should find these insights into the Little House life interesting and uplifting.

# Laura's Love Story

*The lifetime love of Laura Ingalls and Almanzo Wilder*

Real love is sometimes stronger than the romance of fiction. Laura and Almanzo's love is such a story. From an unwanted beau – Almanzo – to a beautiful romance; from the heart wrenching tragedy of losing their home and little boy to heartfelt passion; from trials that most do not endure to a love that endured for a lifetime –

*Laura's Love Story* is the true account of two young people who lived through the most trying troubles to form the most lasting love.

Better than fiction, truer than life, this is the love story that put the jollity in Laura's stories and is the final happy ending to her Little House books.

# The Long, Hard Winter of 1880-81

*What was it Really Like?*

Laura Ingalls Wilder's classic novel *The Long Winter* tells the riveting story of the winter of 1880-81. She wrote of three day blizzards, forty ton trains stuck in the snow, houses buried in snowdrifts and a town that nearly starved.

Just how much of her story was fact, and how much was fiction? Was that winter really that bad, or was it just a typical old time winter stretched a bit to make a good tale?

Author Dan L. White examines the reality of the long, hard winter using contemporary newspaper articles, autobiographies and historical accounts of those who lived through that time to weave a fascinating story of the incredible winter of 1880-81.

# Laura Ingalls Wilder's Most Inspiring Writings
*Notes and Setting by Dan L. White*

These sparkling works of Laura Ingalls Wilder came before she wrote her famous book *Little House on the Prairie*, from which the television show came. The eight other books she wrote tell of her life as a girl on the American frontier between about 1870 and 1889. But years before writing these books, she wrote articles about small farms, country living and just living life for the *Missouri Ruralist* magazine. *Laura Ingalls Wilder's Most Inspiring Writings* is a collection of forty-eight of the most interesting and uplifting of these writings.

Within Laura's words are gems of down to earth wisdom. Amazingly, most of her comments mean just as much today as when she wrote them. These writings give us her philosophy of life and are the seed stock of Laura's prairie books.

# Devotionals with Laura
*Laura Ingalls' Favorite Bible Selections;*
*What they meant in her life, what they might mean in yours*

Laura Ingalls Wilder was a wonderful writer and an eager Bible reader. After her death a list of her most cherished Bible selections was found in her Bible. *Devotionals with Laura* discusses these Bible passages, including:

- How they might have fit in with Laura's life;
- What they might mean in our lives;
- How they affected the Little House books.

When Laura said that she read a certain passage at a time of crisis or discouragement in her life, what events might have caused her to do that? When was she in a crisis? When was she discouraged? What did she say in her writings about such a time?

We include excerpts from Laura's articles where she talked about such events. When we have done these *Devotionals with Laura*, meditated on the passages she meditated on, considered her words for life's critical times, and taken in deeply the very words of Almighty God, then we can begin to understand how Laura's little Bible helped shape the Little House books.

## Big Bible Lessons from Laura Ingalls' Little Books

The Little House books by Laura Ingalls Wilder are lovable, classic works of literature. They contain no violence and no vulgarities, yet they captivate young readers and whole families with their warmth and interest.

They tell the life of young Laura Ingalls, who grew up on the American frontier after the Civil War. Laura was part of a conservative Christian family, and they lived their lives based on certain unchanging values – drawn from the Bible.

*Big Bible Lessons from Laura Ingalls' Little Books* examines the Bible principles that are the foundation of Laura's writing, the Ingalls family, and the Little House books. Not directly stated in words, they were firmly declared in the everyday lives of the Ingalls family. While you enjoy Laura's wonderful books, this book and these Bible lessons will help you and your family also grow spiritually from them.

## The Real Laura Ingalls

*Who was Real, What was Real on her Prairie TV Show*

Fans of the **Little House on the Prairie** TV show know it was taken from Laura Ingalls Wilder's books. They know those books told the real story of Laura's life. But most have never read her books.

Then they wonder —

- What really happened?
- Who was real? Who wasn't?
- What stories on the show were like the stories in her books?

This book tells you just that.

*The Real Laura Ingalls* is for those fans of the show who have never read Laura's books and want to know how the show's stories connect with Laura's real life.

They do connect! From Almanzo to Nellie Oleson to sister Mary, the connection between the show's stories and Laura's stories is a fascinating story in itself. *The Real Laura Ingalls* tells this story in a fast moving, easy reading, crystal clear style, while upholding the values of the show and the books.

## Reading along with Laura Ingalls at her Kansas Prairie Home

*Little House on the Prairie* is the most famous of all the great books by Laura Ingalls Wilder. There she tells how her family traveled to Kansas and built a log house, how Pa almost died digging a well, how they were almost burned out by a prairie wildfire, and how they faced possible attack from wolves and Indians.

*Reading Along with Laura Ingalls at her Kansas Prairie Home* goes along with that book, chapter by chapter, event by event –

and tells more about how it really was –

there in 1870 on that Kansas prairie.

*Little House on the Prairie* deserves more than just a quick read. Such a beloved book stirs thought, reflection and remembering. *Reading Along with Laura Ingalls at her Kansas Prairie Home* does that. Read along with Laura, laugh along with Laura, live along with Laura as we search out the times and spirit of these hardy pioneers. Join in as we stretch out your enjoyment of Laura's book, deepen your understanding of her character, and increase your affection for her wonderful family.

*"Oh Charles!"*

## The Jubilee Principle *God's Plan for Economic Freedom*

WND Books, available at wndbooks.com.

–examines the economic "long wave", a boom-and-bust cycle that happens roughly twice a century in free economies, and parallels the wisdom of the fifty-year Jubilee cycle in the Bible. *The Jubilee Principle* shows how God designed Israel's society with the Sabbath, festivals, land sabbath and Jubilee year. How would it be to live a whole life under that system? *The Jubilee Principle* points the way to true security.

# Life Lessons from Jane Austen's Pride and Prejudice *From her book, her characters and her Bible*

Seven characters in *Pride and Prejudice* –

- Mr. George Wickham, with a most pleasing appearance;
- Miss Jane Bennet, who thought ill of no one and who spoke against no ills;
- Miss Charlotte Lucas, who married for position and got only what she sought;
- Mr. William Collins, whose humble abode was so very close to Rosings Park;
- Miss Elizabeth Bennet, with her consuming search for a man of character;
- and Mr. Fitzwilliam Darcy, who helped her find him –

These seven characters in *Pride and Prejudice* present seven aspects of human nature and the consequent complications of obtaining character, in portrayals that were carefully planned and scripted by Miss Austen. *Life Lessons from Jane Austen's Pride and Prejudice* examines Jane's purposeful plan, searching out the depths of her memorable personalities, and seeking the profundity of her meaningful lessons in life, in morality, and in young love.

Fans of both the *Pride and Prejudice* novel and the movies who appreciated Miss Austen's strong moral values will appreciate this easy flowing study of her comedic characters and her Christian character, making a great love story even better.

# Wifely Wisdom for Sometimes Foolish Husbands

*From Laura Ingalls to Almanzo and Abigail to Nabal*

A Christian wife may be caught between a rock and a hard place. The rock is Christ, the spiritual rock who commands wives to be submissive to their husbands; and the hard place is the husband, who sometimes has less than perfect wisdom. *Wifely Wisdom for Sometimes Foolish Husbands* discusses the pickle of a wife being submissive but still sharing her wisdom with a husband during his few and far-between foolish moments. Such examples include Laura Ingalls sharing her insights with her husband Almanzo Wilder; Ma and Pa Ingalls; and Abigail and Nabal, whose very name meant fool.

This is a sprightly look at a serious subject, when marriage is under attack from all sides as never before. If a wife can share basic wisdom with her husband when he acts like Nabal, then they may save their marriage and rescue their family from destruction. Laura and Almanzo shared good times and bad times, through chucked churns and hot lid lifters, times when she spoke and times when she didn't, times when he listened and times when he didn't, and through all that their marriage lasted for sixty-three years. *Wifely Wisdom for Sometimes Foolish Husbands* may add a few years, or decades, or a lifetime, to your marriage.

# Daring to Love like God

*Marriage as a Spiritual Union*

The *Love Dare* program, made famous in the movie *Fireproof*, was for people whose marriages had problems, to dare them to take steps to better those marriages. *Daring to Love like God* is the next step, for people with good marriages, who are not about to split, who love God and each other, and who want to grow to become a true spiritual union.

This is one of the great miracles in creation: two people, with different abilities, personalities and wants, who become one, with each other and with God. If you want to be challenged to the very best marriage, *Daring to Love like God* leads you up that path.


## School Baals
*How an Old Idol with a New Name Sneaked into Your School*

If you believe in the God of the Bible, that is religion and can't be taught in the government schools.

If you don't believe in the God of the Bible, that is not religion and can be taught in the government schools.

That is also one of the biggest deceptions ever foisted on any people in all of human history.

Idolatry is not just the worship of an idol, but the exalting of the human spirit against its creator. The same human nature that built Baal and made Molech created the anti-God deception that is taught to nine out of ten young people in America. *School Baals* reveals this idolatry in all its duplicity and destruction, and tells you what you can do about it.


## Homeschool Happenings, Happenstance, and Happiness *A Light Look at Homeschool Life*

Homeschool pioneers Margie and Dan White reflect on their homeschool experiences from 1976 until today. With *Homeschool Helpers*, they have held hundreds of homeschool activities and have put out a quarter million words of encouragement. This book includes the top tenth of those writings, everything from homeschooling in the world today to unforgettable family episodes.

Such as –

*"Most people do not see themselves as part of history. If you are a Christian homeschool family, you are part of one of the great religious movements in the history of America, perhaps the greatest. Just as God put the Jews back in the Holy Land, just as He is drawing some Jews to follow Christ, so He is calling you to follow the Messiah directly."*

*"Eventually, as it always does, truth had to prevail. I had half a hot pink truck. I'm not an overly proud man, I wear jeans and drive old vehicles, and this is really laid back country, but there was absolutely no way I was driving that half a hot pink truck into Hartville."*

*"With no institutions supporting it, and all of them opposing it, why in the world did homeschooling grow by perhaps 20% a year?"*

*"We taught all our five kids to read, starting at about age two. We had no idea that they were not "ready to learn." "*

This book is about family, faith and fun –

Homeschool happenings, happenstance, and happiness!


## Tebows' Homeschooled! Should You?
*How Homeschooling put God back in Education!*

Tim Tebow is the world's most famous modern day homeschooler. His parents, Pam and Bob Tebow, homeschooled all five of their children. The intense attention on Tim has also put a spotlight on homeschooling. Although practically everyone in the country now knows about homeschooling, the movement still educates only a few percent of the overall student population. Most people are far more familiar with the factory approach to education than this method of individual tutoring.

Tim Tebow's homeschool education was typical of homeschooling in a number of ways. In some ways, of course, his experience was unique. Yet even in that uniqueness he typifies homeschooling, because homeschooling excels with uniqueness. Therefore, there is much to learn about homeschooling in general by looking at Tim Tebow's homeschooling. In this book, we try to draw out those lessons.

Made in the USA
Monee, IL
17 July 2021